The Behaviour Learning Programme

A collaborative approach to tackling difficult behaviours for schools, parents, carers and pupils.

www.teachingexpertise.com/teachtoinspire

The Behaviour Learning Programme

A collaborative approach to tackling difficult behaviours for schools, parents, carers and pupils.

Colin Boylan

This book is commissioned by Barbara Maines and George Robinson for Teach to Inspire, a series for Optimus Education.

Author:

Colin Boylan

Designer:

Jess Wright

Cover image: ©istockphoto.com/Chris Pike

Editors:

George Robinson and Barbara Maines

Copy Editor:

Mel Maines

Illustrator: Laurie Woodruff

www.lauriewoodruff.com

Printed by: CMP (UK) Ltd.

Registered Office: G3 The Fulcrum, Vantage Way, Poole, Dorset BH12 4NU

Registered Number: 299 7187

Published by Optimus Education: a division of Optimus Professional Publishing Ltd.

Registered Office: 33-41 Dallington Street, London EC1V 0BB

Registered Number: 05791519

Telephone: 0845 450 6407 Fax: 0845 450 6410

www.teachingexpertise.com

ISBN 978-1-906517-14-4

A CD-ROM is attached to the inside front cover and is an integral part of this publication.

Contents

Summary of Contents   3

Introduction   5

Chapter 1 Staff Development for Positive Behaviour Management   15

Chapter 2 PowerPoint Presentation   29

Chapter 3 Introducing the Programme and Pupil Admissions   45

Chapter 4 Parental Involvement   55

Chapter 5 The Choice Programme   63

Chapter 6 After the Programme   141

Bibliography   149

Use of the CD-ROM

Many Teach to Inspire publications include CD-ROMs to support the purchaser in the delivery of the training or teaching activities. These may include any of the following file formats:

- PDFs requiring Acrobat v.3.
- Microsoft Word files.
- Microsoft PowerPoint files.
- Video clips which can be played by Windows Media Player.
- If games are included the software required is provided on the CD-ROM.

All material on the accompanying CD-ROM can be printed by the purchaser/user of the book. This includes library copies. Some of this material is also printed in the book and can be photocopied but this will restrict it to the black and white/greyscale version when there might be a colour version on the CD-ROM.

The CD-ROM itself must not be reproduced or copied in its entirety for use by others without permission from the publisher.

All material on the CD-ROM is © Boylan 2009

 ## Symbol Key

This symbol indicates a page that can be photocopied from the book or printed from the PDF file on the CD-ROM.

Summary of Contents

Introduction

Why the 'Choice' Behaviour Learning Programme was developed and how it fits into current legislation.

Chapter 1 Staff Development for Positive Behaviour Management

This chapter guides staff, by activities, to the realisation that pupil behaviour is best managed through a whole-school approach to positive behaviour strategies. Individual teachers or groups of teachers will find the activities useful as part of individual or departmental development.

Chapter 2 PowerPoint Presentation

The PowerPoint presentation is used as a catalyst for introducing staff to the concept of positive management and as an overview for the Choice Programme.

Chapter 3 Introducing the Programme and Pupil Admissions

It is important that the programme does not become a sin-bin and therefore procedures and structures have to be in place for appropriate pupil admission.

Chapter 4 Parental Involvement

Parental involvement gives us an opportunity to encourage greater and more meaningful partnerships between school, family and community.

Chapter 5 The Choice Programme

After a general introduction and with facilitator notes, the Choice Programme is broken down into the following:

- An initial session where pupils are introduced to the programme.
- A behaviour audit where pupils look at their past behaviours and are introduced to the concepts of ownership and consequences.
- Behaviour activities which are divided into five skills areas:
  1. Concentration.
  2. Listening.
  3. Communication.
  4. Sitting.
  5. Co-operation.
- The programme's sixth skill, 'individual work skills', is incorporated in all of the activities.
- Individual work skills projects are freestanding pieces of work that are designed to encourage, in pupils, a more positive attitude towards their work.
- The final session gives pupils and facilitators an opportunity to evaluate, celebrate and plan for the future.

Chapter 6 After the Programme

How we can support and motivate pupils after the programme when they have returned to class.

Bibliography

Introduction

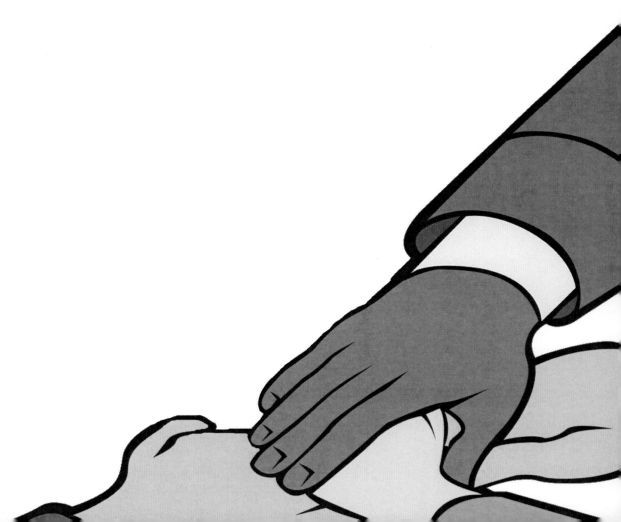

Introduction

The programme of work in this book has developed from a personal belief that children with special needs should be integrated into mainstream schools wherever possible. In 1999, as a member of the senior management team in an 11-16 secondary school in West Belfast, and with 15 years' experience as pastoral assistant head teacher, I was asked to fulfil the role of Special Education Needs Co-ordinator (SENCO).

I accepted this role on the understanding that pupils with behavioural and emotional difficulties would be included, along with pupils who had literacy, numeracy or medical problems, in the categorisation of Special Education Needs.

It was my opinion that pupils exhibiting behaviour difficulties were treated less sympathetically than those with other special needs. If a pupil had difficulty with literacy then a whole raft of strategies was employed to diagnose the specific problem and help the child develop strategies to overcome that difficulty. There was a positive approach to the problem, whereas with behaviour, the majority of strategies were negative. Punishment, suspension and even expulsion seemed to be the only pathways. Even the legislation since 1981 which had promoted the integration and inclusion of a wide range of children in mainstream settings had not specifically included pupils with behavioural problems. Both the 1993 Education Act and the Government Green Paper 'Excellence for All Children' (1997) highlighted commitment to including children with special educational needs wherever possible and removing barriers inherent in integration links.

> 'Qualified duty to secure education of children with special educational needs in ordinary schools.'
>
> (1) Any person exercising any functions under this part of this act in respect of a child with special educational needs who should be educated in a school shall secure that, if the conditions mentioned in subsection (2) below are satisfied, the child is educated in a school which is not a special school unless that is incompatible with the wishes of his parent.
>
> (2) The conditions are that educating the child in a school which is not a special school is compatible with:
>
> (a) his receiving the special education provision which his learning calls for
>
> (b) the provision of efficient education for the children with whom he will be educated and the efficient use of resources.'
>
> (Education Act 1993)

The Code of Practice refers to eight different types of special educational need: a ninth type of special need is not specifically included in the Code but is implicit in its principles and procedures:

1. Learning difficulties.
2. Specific learning difficulties.
3. Emotional and behavioural difficulties.
4. Physical difficulties.
5. Hearing difficulties.
6. Visual difficulties.

7. Speech and language difficulties.

8. Medical conditions.

9. Gifted underachievers (ninth category).

I was of the belief that one of the major challenges facing post-primary schools in implementing an inclusive approach was the provision for their pupils who were experiencing behavioural difficulties. Starting a new behaviour learning programme provided the opportunity to develop new practices and came from the belief that behaviour problems should be approached as a learning difficulty and that schools could set in place learning strategies for pupils with this special educational need.

My starting point for the development of this programme was the findings by the Northern Ireland Training Inspectorate in the 1997/1998 evaluations of the effectiveness and the provision for pupils with emotional and behavioural difficulties (EBD) across the five Education and Library Boards. One of the main findings of the survey was the importance attributed to the promotion of a positive ethos in EBD provision and its influence on the management of behaviour. The key features included:

- the creation of a secure and caring environment

- a commitment to achievement

- the consistent application of rules and routines

- a careful preparation of work by teachers

- a corporate approach to planning

- a clear focus on reintegrating the pupils into mainstream education

- high expectations of the pupils

- external accreditation of pupils' work

- the successful involvement of parents in the pupil's efforts.

'…the development of an ethos in which pupils feel secure, know that they are valued as individuals, and are supported in their learning, personal growth, and social development.'

(1997/1998 N.I. Inspection Report)

The report went on to look at the most effective strategies and programmes that specify clearly how good behaviour was to be encouraged. A school must ensure that:

- clear and comprehensive policy statements are in place

- procedures are clearly understood by all staff and pupils

- a range of strategies is available to meet the needs of the individual pupil

- activities are planned to help the pupils to develop skills they need in order to manage their behaviour better

- individual targets are set and reviewed constantly

- behaviour targets are integrated into teaching and learning

- regular evaluation is effectively implemented.

'...the development of co-ordinated and suitably differentiated programmes and structures, understood by all staff and pupils, to meet the individual educational, emotional, and behaviour needs of the pupils.'

(1997/1998 N.I. Inspection Report)

What I discovered was that the majority of work, research and findings on behaviour were within the EBD environment and not mainstream schooling. In order to identify the problems within a mainstream school I consulted staff and found that what caused most concern was not the one of serious behaviour incident, but rather the constant low-level pupil disruption in class. With agreement from staff I observed lessons and came to the conclusion that a significant number of pupils were being disruptive because they did not know what appropriate behaviour was within the classroom environment. They had not learned the social skills that are needed. As teachers we expect pupils to have already learned these skills in the way we had, in the home environment, but for many that was not the case.

The young boy who was constantly shouting out in class and interrupting the teacher was keen to learn, did not see himself as a behavioural problem, and was becoming more and more frustrated because he thought that the teacher was picking on him. Skills that I had learned as a child, sometimes painfully but never forgotten, had not been learned by these pupils. Old-fashioned maxims, such as:

- Do not talk when an adult is talking.

- Only speak when you are spoken to.

- Sit quietly.

- Do not answer back.

- Sit still.

- Pay attention.

These, along with 'eat your greens' and 'clear your plate', had been learned by my generation at home and then reinforced at school. However outdated that approach may appear now, it gave that generation a selection of skills that would benefit them not only in school but in some workplaces. A large number of our pupils needed to develop similar skills that would help them not only survive within a classroom setting but also maximise their educational opportunities.

After several weeks of classroom observation and with 30 years' classroom practice, I identified six basic classroom skills that every child needed in order to not only fulfil their potential in school but to actually survive in that environment.

1. Concentration.

2. Listening.

3. Communication.

4. Sitting.

5. Co-operation.

6. Individual work skills.

During this period of investigation Goleman (1995) was generating a lot of discussion with his book on emotional intelligence.

'Emotional intelligence refers to the ability to sense, understand, value and effectively apply the power and acumen of emotions as a source of human energy, information, trust, creativity, and influence.'

(Goleman, 1995)

The term 'emotional intelligence' was first introduced in 1990 by Peter Salovey and John Mayer who used it to describe a form of social intelligence that involved the ability to monitor one's own and others' feelings and emotions, to discriminate between them, and to use this information to guide one's thinking and action.

Goleman (1995) categorised five dimensions in developing children's social, emotional and behavioural skills:

1. Self-awareness.

2. Managing feelings.

3. Motivating others.

4. Empathy.

5. Social and interpersonal skills.

Even though Goleman categorised the five dimensions listed above they are often considered to fall into two main categories:

1. The Personal: Self-Awareness.

Self-awareness involves having an accurate understanding of how you behave and how other people perceive your behaviour. It is about being sensitive to your feelings, purpose and general communication style at any given moment in time. Most of all it is about accurately disclosing this awareness to others.

2. The Interpersonal: Social Skills.

That the individual will have the skill and proficiency to induce a desirable response in others.

Recent government initiatives now emphasise the importance of the development of emotional intelligence. The Social and Emotional Aspects of Learning (SEAL) has been described both nationally and internationally by various titles including personal and social development, emotional intelligence, emotional literacy, social and emotional competence, and social and emotional behavioural skills. It is important that we develop these aspects of our curriculum not just for those pupils experiencing difficulties but also for all pupils since these skills:

- underlie almost all aspects of our lives

- enable us to be effective learners

- enable us to get on with other people

- help us become responsible citizens.

'If they [pupils] fail to become contributing adults, these young people represent a very substantial loss of potential to the country, to the economy, to communities and to individual lives.'

(Morris et al.,1999)

The ethos of a behaviour learning programme needed to reflect the school ethos, therefore the programme could not be seen as a detention unit or sin-bin but should offer a teaching and learning environment that would address pupil indiscipline as a learning difficulty. During the development of this programme it was important to remember that it was not an isolated unit, but part of a larger community involving the whole school, that is, staff, parents/carers and pupils. It had to be an integral part of the school community, a learning experience and not somewhere, like a prison, where disruptive children can be sent to serve their time, often doing pointless repetitive rewriting of school rules, before being sent back to class. This was not a simple mathematical model of:

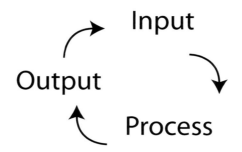

For many pupils with behaviour problems the process became cyclical.

The pupils involved had to learn new skills, make choices on using these skills and, more importantly, carry these new skills and choices into the classroom setting. Equally, if this approach was to be successful the whole school had to have a more positive approach to behavioural issues and parents/carers had to be actively involved as equal partners. Over a one-year period I initiated and led developments in these three areas:

1. Pupils learn new skills.
2. Positive whole-school approach to behaviour.
3. Parents/carers as partners.

Staff development and guidelines on how to manage disruptive pupils were initiated and implemented, the pupil behaviour learning programme, which we called Choice, was formalised and working relationships with parents/carers as equal partners were developed. Together these created an environment with a positive approach to discipline. It allowed the school to live its ethos and mission statement and created a more open environment for teaching and learning. This approach was indeed a practical implementation of the influential Steer Report (2005) which acknowledged that low-level disruption was the main behaviour-related issue facing schools. Steer argued that this low-level disruptive behaviour could create a climate that increased the likelihood of more serious incidents.

The Steer Report stated that good practice should include:

- a consistent approach to behaviour management
- a strong, supportive leadership team which sets high standards
- support and development opportunities for school staff
- involving parents and other agencies
- engaging pupils through good teaching and an appropriate curriculum
- a system of rewards and sanctions

- good pastoral support for pupils
- supporting pupils as they change schools and classes
- good organisation and a high quality environment.

In Managing Challenging Behaviour (2005), Ofsted found that persistent disruptive behaviour is also the most common reason for pupils being excluded from school. It accounted for more than one-fifth of exclusions.

The Choice Programme was developed in order that pupils could learn management and coping skills that would enable them to return to their mainstream classes with the skills necessary for survival in the classroom environment.

'Understanding how to behave has to be taught. Schools must adopt procedure and practices that help pupils learn how to behave appropriately. Good behaviour must be modelled by adults in their interactions with pupils.'

(Steer Report, 2005)

'Learning to behave well is a basic requirement in preparing children to function effectively in communities. Schools with support from others, including parents, have a key role in preparing future citizens.'

(Bell, 2005)

The whole-school positive behaviour approach and subsequent behaviour learning programme were born out of necessity, developed from a practical teaching background, and implemented within a school.

The following chapters give a guide and ideas on how to deliver staff development relating to a positive approach to behaviour management; how to implement the Choice Programme which identifies pupils at risk, teaches them new skills to assist their behaviour with a desired outcome that they will engage positively with their future education, and how to engage parents/carers in supporting their child on the programme and later when their child returns to class.

Chapter 1 Staff Development for Positive Behaviour Management

This chapter guides the staff, by activities, to the realisation that pupil behaviour is best managed through a whole-school approach to positive behaviour strategies. The activities are designed to give staff empowerment, and ownership, of a positive behaviour management system that meets the needs of their school. At the same time individual teachers or groups of teachers will find the activities useful as part of their individual or departmental development.

Chapter 2 PowerPoint Presentation

The PowerPoint presentation is used as a catalyst to introducing school staff to this concept of positive management and as an overview of the behaviour learning programme. In order for the programme to be successful in a school, it is important that all staff, not just those delivering the programme, understand how it fits into the school's overall pastoral provision.

Chapter 3 Introducing the Programme and Pupil Admissions

This shows how the concept was first developed and how it integrates into a school setting. It is important that the programme does not become a sin-bin and therefore procedures and structures have to be in place for pupil admission. These structures and procedures can be adjusted and defined to fit an individual school's pastoral system.

Chapter 4 Parental Involvement

Parental involvement gives us an opportunity to encourage greater and more meaningful partnerships between the school, the family, and the community. As a whole school activity it encourages us to break down barriers, either perceived or real, and create more meaningful relationships between the parent and the teacher.

Chapter 5 The Choice Programme

After a general introduction the Choice Programme is broken down into the following:

- An outlined timetable for the five-day programme.

- An initial session where pupils, usually in groups of six to eight, are introduced to the programme and the future choices they will have if their behaviour continues in its present manner.

- A behaviour audit gets pupils to look at their past behaviours and introduces them to the concepts of ownership and consequences.

- Behaviour activities that are divided into five skills areas:

  1. Concentration.

  2. Listening.

  3. Communication.

  4. Sitting.

  5. Co-operation.

The programme's sixth skill, 'individual work skills', is incorporated in all the activities and projects. These are the skills that each individual pupil will need to improve in order to not only remain in a mainstream class but to make the most of their education.

- The projects are freestanding pieces of work that allow the pupil an opportunity to produce a finished piece of work that can be displayed. They are designed to encourage in pupils a more positive attitude towards their work.

- The final session allows pupils and facilitators an opportunity to evaluate pupil progress, to celebrate pupil achievements and to plan for the future.

Chapter 6 After the Programme

When pupils have completed the programme and returned to mainstream class they will need support and motivation not only from the facilitator involved but from everyone in the school community, especially class teachers and parents/carers. The pupil has not changed overnight into a perfect pupil but has made a positive choice about their future. With the support of a target diary and facilitator mentoring, this positive future can be achieved and supported.

Chapter 1

Staff Development for Positive Behaviour Management

Chapter 1 Staff Development for Positive Behaviour Management

Introduction

The behaviour learning programme started from a personal belief that behaviour problems should be approached as a learning difficulty and that schools, under the terms of the Code of Practice, should set in place learning strategies for pupils with this special educational need. The programme focuses on developing skills that the pupil needs in order to become motivated in class and therefore become an effective learner. The programme does not and cannot work in isolation and the whole school community must make an informed choice to adopt a more positive approach towards discipline.

If a school wants to provide a more positive approach to discipline and deliver an effective behaviour learning programme the following choices have to be made:

- Provide a suitable environment for the entire education process.
- Promote good relationships throughout the school.
- Foster and nourish the gifts and abilities of both staff and pupils.
- Make all new pupils and staff feel welcome and valued as members of the school community.
- Encourage loyalty and respect for school, family and community.
- Promote pupils' self-image and self-esteem.
- Develop attitudes of respect, tolerance and honesty.
- Promote the rights of the individual.
- Promote self-discipline along with a positive attitude towards authority.
- Develop in the pupils a sense of responsibility towards society and the preservation of the environment.

Starting the programme goes hand in hand with creating a whole-school positive discipline environment.

> 'The network of relationships and expectations amongst and between pupils, staff, parents, and outside professionals, and the overall quality of pastoral care policies, are as influential in determining this climate as the impact of the formal curriculum and the skills of those who administer it.'

(Charlton and David, 1993)

In terms of pupil behaviour the relationship between the pupil and the teacher is the most important relationship in the school organisation. The way in which teachers model behaviour towards others, and in particular to pupils in their care, is essentially the key factor in creating an atmosphere in which positive behaviour can take place. In such a school, strategies are used to deal with the act of misbehaviour in an appropriate way rather than dealing with the person, the pupil, in what can often be an inappropriate way.

We should always remember that all children have the potential, from time to time, to misbehave. It is also a fact that all teachers will at some time experience behaviour problems in their class. This doesn't make you a bad teacher, but doing nothing about it does, since classroom management is a skill that can be learned and developed.

Staff Development

Along with the PowerPoint presentation on introducing the behaviour learning programme, it may be useful for school-based staff to participate in the following six activities that highlight a positive approach to school disciplinary matters. This is just a starting point for staff to think about explicit expectations regarding positive behaviour and is not intended to be staff development on all aspects of behaviour management. A minority of pupils will be on and benefit from the programme, but for the majority clear, effective and consistent management will not only improve general behaviour, it will also have a major impact on the overall climate of the school. These activities are therefore establishing a starting point to consider behaviour management at a whole-school level. Staff training and development should be introduced in tandem with the pupil programme and could be delivered by a senior pastoral manager in conjunction with the school SENCO. When introducing this positive approach I used a staff training day in order that staff would have sufficient time to discuss and formulate ideas that would lead to future development. I have used this whole-day approach to good effect in other schools where the staff formed working groups to ensure that the school's approach to positive discipline would be on-going. With time being a major consideration in school planning, another consideration for staff development is to stagger it, using one afternoon per week, over a half term period.

The Activities

Activity 1 Unacceptable Behaviour

'All children need to know the boundaries that are expected of them and the confines they can work in. What is acceptable behaviour and what is not?'

Facilitator Notes

This activity requires the staff to be placed in cross-curricular groups of seven to ten and to consider what unacceptable behaviour is for their school. Staff can consider the levels of misbehaviour under the headings Minor, Serious and Very Serious.

What is their role as classroom teachers in regard to sanctions and strategy?

Who should accept responsibility for managing serious and very serious misbehaviour?

The activity page, Unacceptable Behaviour, at the end of this chapter could be used to record discussion. Take feedback and discuss.

What does this suggest about their school systems and the present provision for pupils with behavioural difficulties?

Activity 2 Class Code of Conduct

'Good individual and class behaviour starts with the class teacher having clear expectations for the pupils that are explicit and illustrated with appropriate examples.'

Facilitator Notes

Staff can discuss and agree upon a general class code of conduct, the activity page at the end of this chapter could be used to record discussion.

Examples:

- Establish a few simple class rules. These will form the basis of a code of conduct.
- In order to give ownership, the teacher should develop this process with the children.
- Go over the rules and illustrate what they mean in real terms.
- Phrases like 'show respect' are meaningless. Children need to know what respect looks like, feels like and sounds like.
- Be specific. Explain in simple language in order that the children know exactly what is expected of them.
- Keep revisiting and reinforcing the rules. Go back to the rules time and time again. Remember children can and will forget rules.
- Be positive. Praise the children when they remember and apply the class rules.
- Do not allow transgressions to pass unnoticed. Children will interpret this as condoning bad behaviour.

- Model good behaviour. The use of your children illustrating the rules on posters and photographs is a very positive reinforcement.

When taking feedback it is important for the class teacher to remember that rewards always work best. It is positive behaviour you want to reinforce and encourage, therefore rewarding the class, the group or the individual will highlight the positive while minimising the negative.

Activity 3 Classroom Routines

'All pupils need to know what is expected of them and why. The class teacher should establish clear classroom routines for pupils.'

Facilitator Notes

Staff can discuss what classroom routines can be employed in all classes and how these can be established across the whole school. The activity page at the end of this chapter could be used to record discussion.

For example, routines for:
- registration
- entering and leaving the room
- movement in and around the classroom
- giving out equipment and materials
- quiet working
- seeking help if they do not know what to do
- what to do when they have finished their work
- answering questions in class
- homework
- lining up and moving around the school.

The teacher should constantly go back over the routines with the pupils and they should be rewarded for doing the 'right' thing. Time spent establishing and re-establishing class rules and routines is never wasted time.

Activity 4 What Brings Changes in Behaviour?

'Punishments often serve only to help prevent a behaviour occurring in the future; by themselves they do not provide alternative acceptable behaviours which should be used.'

(Charlton and David, 1993)

This behaviour learning programme is built around the assumption that punishments do not bring about real changes in behaviour. Changes in behaviour are achieved through learning and from forming positive relationships.

What are the merits of a positive reward system?

How can we establish in our school a more proactive approach to whole-school behaviour?

Facilitator Notes

In small groups discuss some of the following:

- Research, across the years and in many different cultures and countries, has always shown that rewards work best.

- Punishment regimes do not change attitudes and they do not change behaviours.

- Reward all children and reward them often for good behaviour. Do not fall into the negative thinking trap that all children are supposed to behave well, so good behaviour, as opposed to good work, should go unrewarded.

- Have differentiated rewards as well as differentiated teaching. If you want to over-reward a pupil who has behavioural learning difficulties do so, but explain to the class why and encourage their help and support.

- A powerful reward for a child is to have a favourable report sent home. It is often the case that the only communication between the teacher and the parent is concerning negative behaviours.

- Being positive will not only motivate the pupil but will also motivate the parent and establish a greater trust and bond between the school and the home.

Activity 5 Visual Reminders (Classroom)

In small groups discuss the following statement: 'Posters are a positive way of reinforcing classroom rules.'

Create and design posters that will stimulate pupils while at the same time reinforce not only the rule but why we have the rule. The activity page at the end of the chapter could be used for first drafts.

Facilitator Notes

The facilitator should emphasise that the standard way of having a list of rules at the front of a classroom is not meeting the requirements of today's pupils. Pupils are stimulated visually and a coloured poster informing them to have 'Respect for other Pupils' has a more positive influence than a long list of do's and don'ts at the front of the room.

> # Respect
>
> Respect for others in this room means:
> Getting on quietly with work.
> Asking for assistance by raising your hand.
> Respecting others' property.
> Respecting others' feelings.
> Respecting others' right to learn.

If a pupil is being disruptive it gives the teacher an opportunity of challenging the behaviour by referring to the poster.

'Because of your behaviour you are not allowing other pupils to learn.'

'Because you are talking you are not allowing me to teach pupils who are interested in learning.'

This approach depersonalises the negative behaviours we want to eliminate and at the same time gives meaning to the conditions we want to encourage. With this approach all pupils can learn self-respect as well as understanding respect for others involved in the same learning environment.

The following is an example that could be used to stop pupils shouting out in class.

Getting Attention

In our room,

When we wish to ask a question,

We will put up our hands,

And wait our turn.

This gives everyone a chance to speak.

It clearly tells the pupil what is expected and why we behave in this way.

We could create posters for 'Respect for pupils', 'Respect for teachers', 'Safety in the classroom', 'The rights of other pupils to learn', 'The rights of teachers to teach' – the list is endless. School departments could reinforce the school rules by agreeing on a specific rule each month and introducing a poster highlighting that rule in each classroom.

Activity 6 Visual Reminders (School)

In small groups discuss how we can make our general school rules more stimulating and meaningful for our pupils.

Create and design a second set of posters for general use around the school. These posters should emphasise how we behave in our school. The activity page at the end of the chapter could be used for first drafts.

Facilitator Notes

The second set of posters is for general school use in corridors, stairs and so on. If we construct a concept of community and how our community works together then it takes the personalising out of minor incidents and places a greater emphasis on 'how we do things in our school'. This approach also fosters a greater feeling of belonging to and ownership of the school by the pupils.

If a pupil is running or being rowdy in a corridor we can shout at the pupil to stop running or to be quiet. This can often lead to an escalation of the situation and with an audience present can quickly develop into a more serious incident. With the posters prominently displayed in the corridors the teacher or supervisor can quietly explain that shouting or running in the corridor isn't what we do in our school. In this approach the posters reinforce the message and become a learning experience.

When I first introduced this approach, because our own pupils' photographs were used as examples in the posters there was great interest from the entire student body. If the pupils are looking at the photographs on the posters they are also looking at the message the poster is communicating. The following year I used the photographs of new entry pupils on the posters. This had a positive effect on the transfer from primary to post-primary for these pupils, making them feel an integral part of the school community.

When employing this strategy we must remember that as a learning experience it will take time to consolidate, all staff must help with reinforcing a positive approach. Parental permission is needed before pupils' photographs are displayed.

Unacceptable Behaviour

Categorise unacceptable behaviour.

Minor	Serious	Very Serious

What is your role as a classroom teacher in regard to sanctions and strategy?

Who should be responsible for managing serious and very serious misbehaviour?

Class Code of Conduct

Be as specific as you can, what does 'show respect' mean in behavioural terms?

It might include tone of voice, use of correct name, open body language.

1.

2.

3.

4.

5.

6.

7.

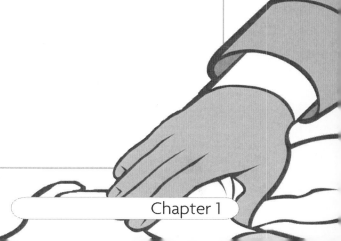

Classroom Routines

What routines do you currently use?

What routines might you use?

Poster for Classroom Rules

Use this sheet for ideas for a first draft of a classroom poster.

Poster for School Rules

Use this sheet for ideas for a first draft of a poster that could be used around the school.

Chapter 2

PowerPoint Presentation

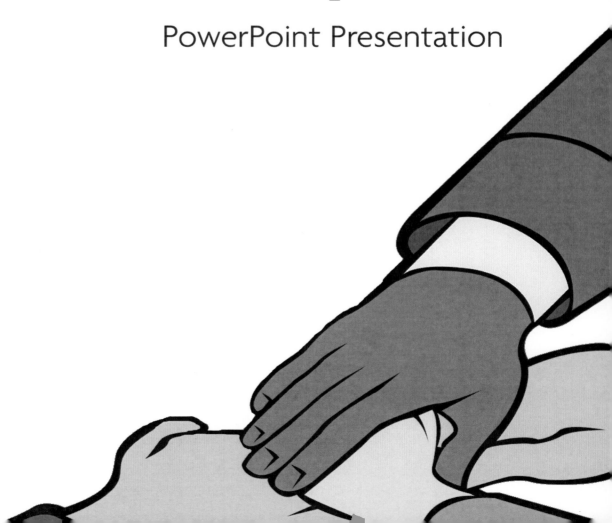

Chapter 2 PowerPoint Presentation

This section provides a PowerPoint presentation with additional notes to support a facilitator in delivering the presentation to staff, governors and, if appropriate, parents/carers about the Choice Programme.

The script is not 'fixed' and can be modified to suit the needs of any school.

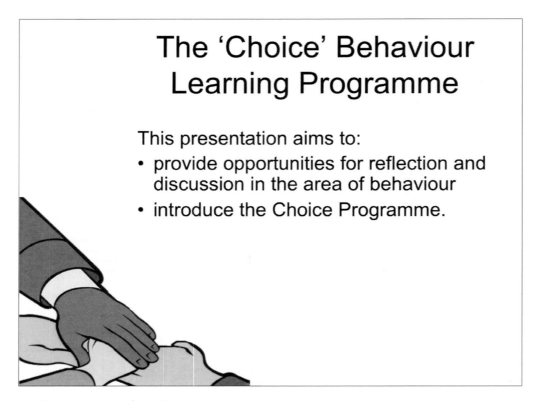

The 'Choice' Behaviour Learning Programme

This presentation aims to:
- provide opportunities for reflection and discussion in the area of behaviour
- introduce the Choice Programme.

Facilitator Notes for Slide 1

This school has many examples of good practice. Today gives us a time for reflecting on managing behaviour, to look at what works and what is really going well. It is a time to share ideas and experiences. Teaching has long been known as the lonely profession and today gives us the opportunity to touch base with our colleagues for mutual support. With no National Curriculum on managing behaviour we need to be proactive and not reactive.

As part of that proactive approach we will look at introducing the 'Choice' Behaviour Learning Programme to our school. The Choice Programme was developed so that pupils who are experiencing behavioural difficulties in the classroom can develop the skills necessary for them to make positive choices about their future education and therefore maximise their education potential.

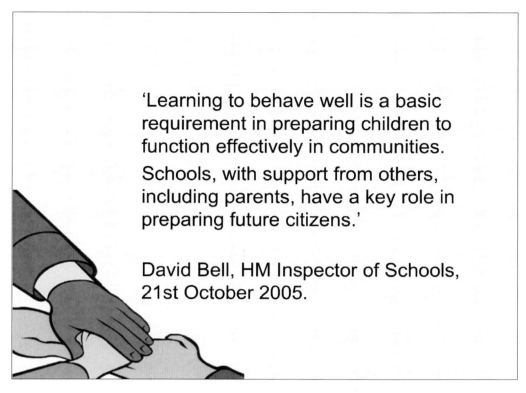

'Learning to behave well is a basic requirement in preparing children to function effectively in communities.

Schools, with support from others, including parents, have a key role in preparing future citizens.'

David Bell, HM Inspector of Schools, 21st October 2005.

Facilitator Notes for Slide 2

Understanding how to behave has to be taught. Schools need to adopt procedures and practices that will help pupils to learn how to behave properly.

It is not enough to expect all our pupils to have developed the skills that enable them to behave well. We, as educators, have to teach and then reinforce these skills. Class and whole-school rules must be fully explained. It is not enough to state the rule and the consequences of rule breaking, we must explain why we have the rule and how breaking the rule has consequences not only for the pupil involved but for everyone in the wider school community.

We, as teachers, have to realise that we do not work in isolation and that alone we cannot be expected to have all the answers to pupil behavioural issues. We are part of a community of teachers and should draw from the experience and expertise of our colleagues. Likewise the school cannot work in isolation and must work in co-operation with the wider community of parents/carers and outside agencies.

This collective co-operative approach, along with the example of good behaviour modelled by adults in their interactions with our pupils, highlights the school's positive, proactive approach to discipline.

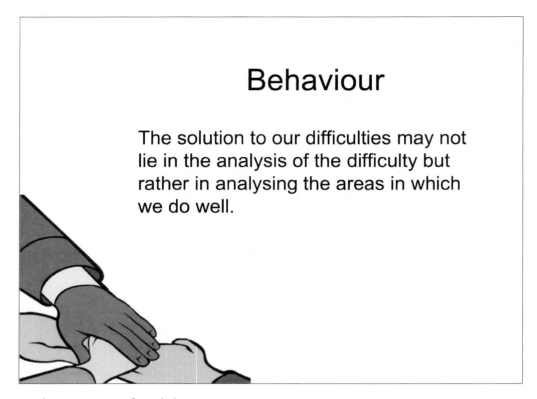

Behaviour

The solution to our difficulties may not lie in the analysis of the difficulty but rather in analysing the areas in which we do well.

Facilitator Notes for Slide 3

It is important that as a school we have an agreed approach to dealing with disruptive behaviour. The behaviour issues identified as having an impact on our school on a day-to-day basis can be categorised under the three headings:

1. Minor.

2. Serious.

3. More serious.

The activity page 'Unacceptable Behaviour' from Chapter 1 could be used if appropriate. We can then identify best practice from our school in dealing with these behaviours in order that best practice is universally accepted and delivered. The school needs to have a clear, understandable and workable referral system that is administered by all staff and understood by pupils. Who deals with a situation? Is it the subject teacher, the form or year head or head teacher? What actions can and should be taken? It is vital that these agreed referrals and actions to be taken are discussed and agreed in the light of a positive behaviour framework and that flexibility is built into the system. As teachers, if a pupil has been referred to the next level we must respect the professionalism of our colleague dealing with the issue.

Activity Linked to Slide 3

In small groups or in departmental groups discuss the following:

• What behaviour issues impact on our school on a day-to-day basis?

• What do you think some of the causes are?

• What does the school currently do well in managing behaviour?

The 'Behaviour' activity page could be used to record the discussion.

The Choice Programme for Pupils

The aim of the programme is to help pupils to develop into self-disciplined individuals who understand their own and others' feelings.

- We want our pupils to be self-aware.
- We want our pupils to accept responsibility for their actions.
- We want our pupils to accept the consequences of their actions.
- We want our pupils to link their actions to emotions and feelings.

Facilitator Notes for Slide 4

The Choice Programme began from a belief that pupil behavioural problems should be approached as a learning difficulty and that schools, under the terms of the Code of Practice, should set in place learning strategies for pupils with this special educational need. Why should pupils with behaviour difficulties be treated in a less positive manner than pupils with literacy, numeracy or medical difficulties? The programme focuses on the skills that are needed for a pupil to become motivated to learn and therefore progress within the school environment. It emphasises structures that develop greater involvement with parents and carers, encourages target setting, develops greater staff involvement, involves pupils in decision-making and in taking ownership of their future behaviour. It was designed to help pupils to achieve a level of classroom management skills in order to remain in a mainstream class. It is a holistic approach that offers advice and practical guidance in order that schools become more proactive in their approach to positive behaviours, putting their ethos into practice and developing partnerships with parents/carers.

Activity Linked to Slide 4

Discuss in small groups the additional strategies used in our school to help pupils to overcome difficulty with literacy.

- What strategies do we employ for pupils with behavioural difficulties?

- Are all our strategies positive and do they make learning more meaningful?

The 'Changing Behaviour' activity page from the end of this chapter could be used to record the discussion.

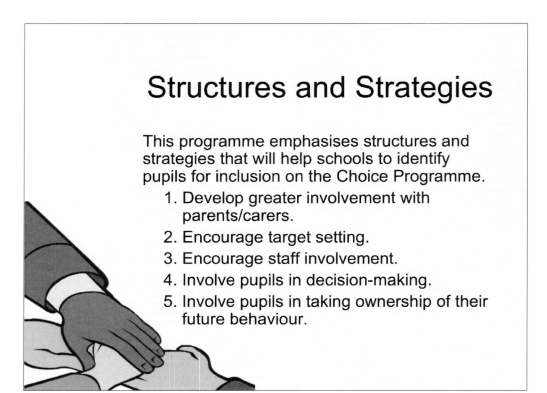

Structures and Strategies

This programme emphasises structures and strategies that will help schools to identify pupils for inclusion on the Choice Programme.

1. Develop greater involvement with parents/carers.
2. Encourage target setting.
3. Encourage staff involvement.
4. Involve pupils in decision-making.
5. Involve pupils in taking ownership of their future behaviour.

Facilitator Notes for Slide 5

This programme has been developed in order to help pupils to develop the skills necessary not only to remain in a mainstream class but also to maximise their potential. It is important to understand that the programme is not a 'dumping ground' or 'sin-bin'. Pupil behaviour issues should initially be addressed by the subject teacher and when the issues become more serious should be referred under the system agreed by the school. The form teacher/year head, in consultation with the subject teacher, will be the normal route onto the programme.

When a pupil has been admitted onto the programme there will be greater parental involvement. Parents/carers will be encouraged to attend programme sessions whenever possible and will have to monitor and sign daily reports and target diaries. The target diary will be introduced to the pupil when they are returning to mainstream class. The subject teacher will be involved with the target diary and will have to sign it at the end of each lesson, indicating if the pupil has achieved the agreed targets. In general the programme encourages the pupil to make positive decisions regarding future behaviour and when the pupil returns to mainstream class the subject teacher, by positive motivation, helps the pupil to achieve the agreed targets.

Skills for All

- The programme was developed to help pupils whose behaviours were leading them towards suspension and expulsion.
- The programme was designed for pupils at risk of missing a mainstream education.
- The skills and awareness activities used on the programme, in order to help pupils become motivated to learn and therefore progress within the school environment, can be used with all pupils in any school.

Facilitator Notes for Slide 6

- Does the difficult pupil have effective means of communicating with others?

- Does the pupil know what's expected? For example, we may demand an apology but the pupil may not be aware that she has done something wrong.

- Does the pupil have experience of making choices in his life?

- Does the pupil have regular opportunities for positive feedback and reinforcement?

- Does the pupil have appropriate social skills?

The Choice Programme has identified the skills needed by a pupil in a classroom setting and has developed activities that will introduce and reinforce these skills.

The Choice Programme Identifies:

- listening skills
- communication skills
- concentration skills
- sitting skills
- co-operation and team or group skills for working with others
- individual work skills, project work.

These skills are added to the concepts of:

- responsibility
- consequences
- ownership.

Facilitator Notes for Slide 7

It is wrong to assume that all pupils have the same developed social skills. These skills have to be taught. Far too often pupils respond in an inappropriate way because they do not fully understand why or for what they are being disciplined. The skills many teachers learned within the home environment at an early age have not been learned by these pupils. If schools are developing young people for adult life then instead of punishing these pupils and in doing so reinforcing negative behaviours, we should be offering a learning environment that will help the pupil make positive choices.

There is a difference between a pupil who doesn't know how to behave properly in a given situation and a pupil who does know and chooses to misbehave.

The programme gives the pupil the skills or the tools but it is the pupil who will choose how to use them.

The Programme Centres on Pupil Choice

Key features include the following:
- Creation of a secure and caring environment.
- Consistent application of rules and routines.
- Commitment to achievement.
- High expectation of pupils.
- Range of strategies available to meet the needs of the individual pupil.
- Activities planned to help pupils to develop the skills they need in order to manage their classroom behaviour.
- Involvement of parents/carers.
- Whole-school approach.

Facilitator Notes for Slide 8

The programme is designed to stimulate pupils' thinking skills and to help pupils to make better, more informed choices with regard to future behaviour. It is important that the programme is delivered in a pleasant environment. It should be non-judgemental. During the programme pupils will exhibit challenging behaviour and these situations should be seen as a learning opportunity and not disciplined in a negative manner.

The programme activities will lead the pupils through challenging behaviour and give them the skills to make informed choices with regard to future behaviours. From the start of the programme there must be a commitment from pupils and programme staff to work together to achieve change. This can only be achieved in the long-term with support from parents/carers and a whole-school commitment to positive discipline.

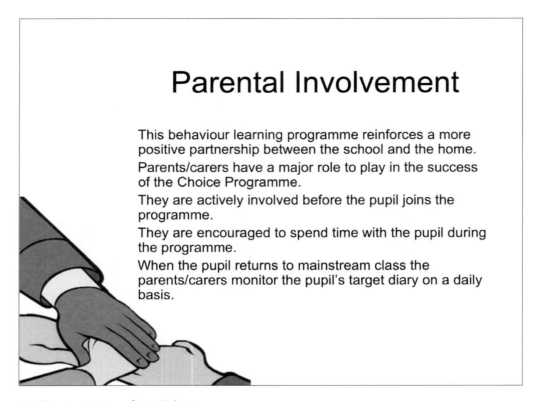

Parental Involvement

This behaviour learning programme reinforces a more positive partnership between the school and the home.

Parents/carers have a major role to play in the success of the Choice Programme.

They are actively involved before the pupil joins the programme.

They are encouraged to spend time with the pupil during the programme.

When the pupil returns to mainstream class the parents/carers monitor the pupil's target diary on a daily basis.

Facilitator Notes for Slide 9

Without positive involvement from the parent or carer the pupil will find it more difficult to make positive choices for his future behaviour.

This involvement has to be directed by the school and the partnership with parents/carers developed. Many parents will feel that they have nothing to offer in the education of their child. It is a priority of the school to encourage these parents, help them to overcome their fears and become actively involved in the education of their children.

The parents/carers will meet with school staff before the pupil is accepted on to the Choice Programme. The pupil will only gain entry to the programme if both the parent/carer and the pupil choose to be fully committed to the work involved.

During the programme the parent/carer is encouraged to join the teaching sessions and to visit the class at any time. This creates ownership and a shared partnership for the parent.

When the pupil returns to the mainstream class the parent monitors the target diary each evening and communicates with school staff.

The Target Diary

For some pupils the target diary becomes an essential part of school life.

It is a contract or agreement between the school, the home and the pupil.

The diary will contain three targets agreed by the school, the parent and the pupil.

The pupil's performance in class will be measured against these targets.

The parent or carer agrees to monitor the diary daily and to discuss with the pupil how they are coping in school, to encourage and praise on progress made, and to contact the school immediately should any difficulties arise.

Facilitator Notes for Slide 10

The target diary allows the pupil to return to class with a new and more realistic start.

Nobody will change into a perfect pupil overnight. Setting realistic targets gives the pupil the opportunity to enjoy success if the effort is made to realise the targets. The use of the target diary must be incorporated in to a whole-school policy on positive behaviour. If we can highlight the small advances made by our pupils then these can lead to more significant positive behaviour changes. At the beginning the class teacher has to concentrate on the pupil achieving the agreed targets, praise the pupil for making these targets and not emphasise any other negative behaviour that might have occurred. A long journey consists of a lot of short steps and the first one is the most important.

You might want to give an example of the target diary which can be found at the end of Chapter 6. A description of the type of targets which should be set is explained in the same chapter.

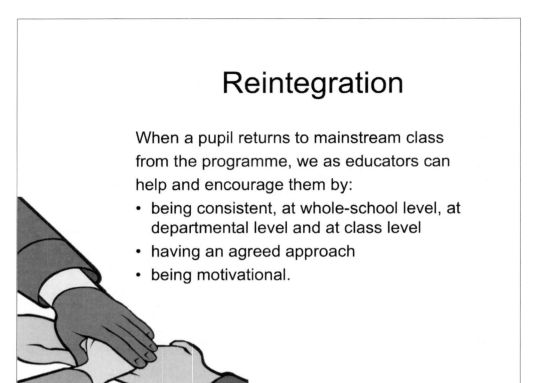

Reintegration

When a pupil returns to mainstream class from the programme, we as educators can help and encourage them by:

- being consistent, at whole-school level, at departmental level and at class level
- having an agreed approach
- being motivational.

Facilitator Notes for Slide 11

In order to have a consistent approach to positive behaviour management we have to have agreement. Our class rules must be few in number and formed in a positive manner. The class rules must be the same and administered in the same way for all classes. Departments across the school must have an agreed strategy to behavioural issues and standards. Departmental policies must have a whole-school approach. What is expected in one department must be accepted for all departments. Above all, we as educators must be motivational.

We must always remember that both positive and negative attention and behaviours can be reinforced and our aim should be to remove reinforcement from inappropriate behaviours while catching moments of appropriate behaviour that can be praised and reinforced.

Behaviour

What behaviour issues impact on our school on a day-to-day basis?

What do you think some of the causes are?

What does the school currently do well in managing behaviour?

Changing Behaviour

What strategies are employed to help students to overcome difficulty with literacy?

What strategies do we employ for pupils with behavioural difficulties?

Are all our strategies for behaviour positive and do they make learning more meaningful?

Chapter 3

Introducing the Programme and Pupil Admissions

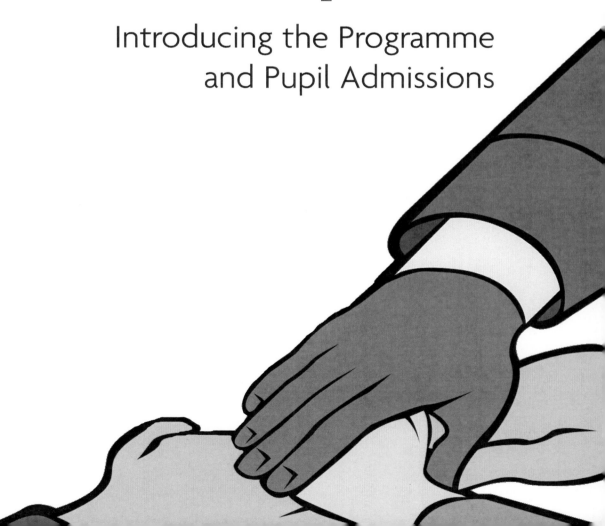

Chapter 3 Introducing the Programme and Pupil Admissions

The Choice Programme was designed in order to help pupils to achieve a level of personal classroom management skills that would enable them to return to class.

The programme identifies:

- concentration skills
- listening skills
- communcation skills
- sitting skills
- co-operation and team or group skills for working with others
- individual work skills.

Added to the above skills are the concepts of responsibilities, consequences, ownership of behaviour and ownership of work. These concepts are reflected in the skills activities and it is important that the programme facilitator emphasise these during each session.

Pupil Choice

The programme centres on pupil choice. There is a difference between a pupil who doesn't know how to behave properly, in a given situation, and a pupil who does know and chooses to misbehave. The programme introduces pupils to the skills, or the tools, necessary to not only survive but to achieve success in a classroom setting, but ultimately it is the pupil who will choose whether to make use of these skills or not.

The programme focuses on the skills that are needed in order that a pupil can not only survive in a main class setting but will also become motivated to learn and therefore progress within that environment. During the programme the pupils are encouraged to look at their rights, face up to their responsibilities and make positive choices.

Pupils' Rights

- The right to an appropriate education.
- The right to be taught without being kept back by others.
- The right to be treated fairly and equally no matter what gender or ability.
- The right to feel safe and secure at all times in the school environment.
- The right not to be bullied.

Pupils' Responsibilities

- To treat all pupils, teachers and other staff with respect.
- To ensure that the school is a safe place to be.
- To attend school regularly and on time.
- To behave correctly especially during teaching and learning.

- To work to the best of one's ability.
- To respect school property.
- To follow the rules of the school.

It is not enough for pupils to know what their individual rights are. They must be made aware that with rights come responsibilities and that their actions cannot take away the rights of others. Pupils do not exist alone and their individual actions and the consequences of these actions affect other members of the community.

Key features of the programme include:

- creation of a secure and caring environment
- commitment to achievement
- consistent application of rules and routines
- a whole-school approach on positive discipline
- high expectation of the pupils
- clear focus on re-integrating pupils into mainstream class
- involvement of parents/carers
- a range of strategies available to meet the needs of the individual pupil
- activities planned to help pupils develop skills they need in order to manage their classroom behaviour.

The programme is organic and will develop to meet the needs of the individual pupil. Working through an activity will often lead in a new direction. The experienced programme facilitator should not be totally rigid, sticking only to the script but should have the confidence to develop new ideas if and when a situation arises. It is important that these new paths are allowed to be developed.

The programme helps to develop structures that will help schools to identify pupils who are having difficulty in class and emphasises the pupil as part of a wide community of support by:

- developing greater involvement with parents/carers
- encouraging target setting
- encouraging staff involvement in positive behaviour management
- involving pupils in decision-making
- involving pupils in taking ownership of future behaviour.

Structure of the Programme

The programme, although originally designed as a one-week intensive course for pupils who were in the process of being excluded from mainstream schooling due to constant and/or persistent behaviour difficulties, can be adapted to meet the needs of schools and specific pupils. The materials can be modified to specific individual and school circumstances and used in differing formats.

- A one-week intensive course – the programme can be delivered over a one-week period to a group of six to eight pupils who have been identified by the school as being difficult and disruptive. I believe that the interaction and discussion by these pupils during this week maximises the programme's benefits.

- Class activity – the programme materials can be tailored to meet the collective needs of a class that is perceived as being disruptive or difficult.

- Small groups – if a school cannot facilitate a complete one-week course then small groups of pupils, five to six in number, who are having behavioural problems can be timetabled either daily or weekly to complete the programme. Using this format the course teacher or tutor can tailor the weekly targets to match the topics covered.

- Individual pupil – for various reasons an intensive one-week course may not meet the needs of a particular pupil. The pupil could complete the programme over an agreed period of time. If the pupil is experiencing behavioural difficulties during particular subjects, periods, or with individual teachers, then this time could be used and would also act as a 'time out' for the pupil, other pupils in the class and the class teacher.

The concept of the programme is to work with pupils who can be turned around and who with the appropriate skills can maximise their educational experiences in the mainstream setting. It must be stated, even at this early stage, that there will be pupils who after completing the programme will still not be best suited to a mainstream educational setting and whose education would be best served in a more specialist environment.

Prior to Admission

It is vital that prior to admission onto the programme all appropriate strategies have been implemented at the various stages. The programme has been designed to run in conjunction with a pastoral system and not instead of it. Since the programme works within a school's pastoral system it is important that all teachers keep records of a child's behaviour history and the strategies the teacher has used in order to help the child overcome any difficulties. It is the normal practice, in the majority of schools, when classroom strategies such as moving the pupil to another seat, talking to the pupil with regard to the difficulty, giving the pupil extra work, detention during break/lunchtime, getting in contact with the parent, have been exhausted then the teacher passes the difficulty up the pastoral chain. It is hoped that when the pupil is passed to the year head or head of department the pupil will realise the seriousness of the situation and decide not to act in that manner again. Unfortunately in that model we have not addressed the needs of the pupil. We have not ascertained why the pupil is behaving in this way and we have not helped the pupil with success strategies for the future. The programme as a special needs strategy gives the child a learning situation to develop skills that can be effectively employed in future classroom settings.

Selecting the Students

For the programme to maximise pupil potential it is essential that it does not become a 'dumping ground' or 'sin-bin'. Entry on to the programme must be regulated. All other classroom strategies must have been previously employed.

When a school is using the programme then pupils' names for admission must be discussed and agreed prior to admission. I have used an admissions panel consisting of year heads, SENCO, assistant head and head who consider names of pupils for admission onto the programme prior to admission in order that parental permission and support can be obtained.

Pupil Information

The 'Pupil Information' sheet (page 51) can be used to show a history of the pupil's behaviour and the strategies employed by the school to help overcome these difficulties.

Admissions Meeting

The Pupil Information sheet and its information would be collated by the pupil's head of year and presented at the admissions meeting. After discussing the case for admission, if it is decided that a non-referral outcome to the programme is in the best interests of the pupil, then it is vital that alternative strategies are identified and put in place. In a way this becomes a safety valve to ensure that the programme does not become a dumping ground or sin-bin and ensures that class teachers and year heads have used all the strategies at their disposal to help the pupil to overcome their difficulties. It is important that the class teacher uses the strategies available to manage misbehaviour in class. At the conclusion of the admissions meeting the information sheet 'Admissions Meeting', page 52, is completed and it is agreed who will oversee and evaluate the effectiveness of the proposed strategies that have been recommended.

Parent/Pupil Meeting

When it has been agreed that inclusion onto the programme would benefit a pupil then initial contact can be made with the parent or carer. This is best done by the school's SENCO during an informal telephone call, at which time the SENCO can explain the benefits of the programme and arrange an informal meeting, possibly in the pupil's home, and a more formal meeting later in the school.

Parental involvement is encouraged at a strategy meeting prior to the pupil's admission onto the programme. These meetings give the school the opportunity to openly discuss the problems encountered to date and how the school, the pupil and the parent/carer can work together to plan a new way forward. The information sheet 'Parent/Pupil Meeting' (page 53) is used to record agreed targets and is signed by the pupil, the parent/carer and the school. These targets should be specific to the pupil's behaviour difficulties, they should be realistic for the pupil to achieve and progress should be easy to measure or observe. The targets agreed are for the duration of the programme but can be changed if the school, the pupil and the parent collectively decide that new targets would help the pupil to achieve greater success.

It is vital that all partners to this agreement want a new future and want to see progress. During the programme communication with the parents in the form of direct contact using daily progress reports is essential. When the pupil is reintegrated back into mainstream class the parents are asked to monitor and sign a daily target diary.

Chapter 6 provides more detail on setting targets.

Pupil Information

Pupil's Name:

Class:

Date:

Form Teacher

Behavioural History

Strategies Used

Year Head

Behavioural History

Strategies Used

Parental Involvement

Form Teacher

Year Head

Outside Agencies' Involvement

Admissions Meeting

Pupil's Name:

Class:

Date:

Comments

Year Head

Assistant Head

Behaviour Unit

SENCO

Others

Outcome: Referral /Non-Referral

Other Strategies to be Used

Non-Referral

Person monitoring strategies

Referral

Parental Meeting

Start Date

Other comments

Signed:

Date:

Parent/Pupil Meeting

Pupil's Name:

Class:

Date:

Brief History

Agreed Targets

Date for Review Meeting

Signed

Parent/Carer

Pupil

School

Date

Chapter 4

Parental Involvement

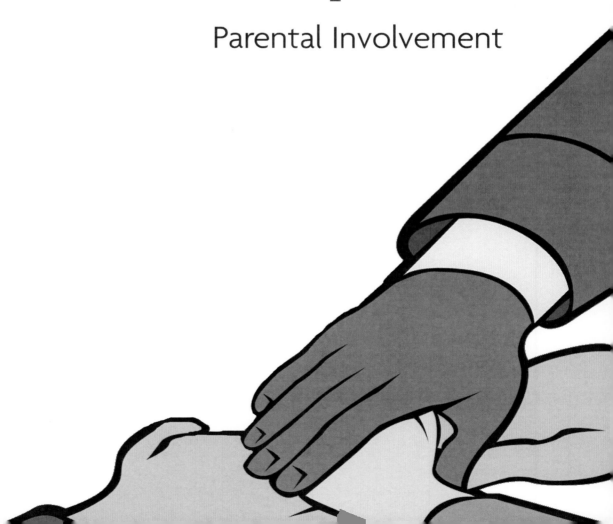

Chapter 4 Parental Involvement

Creating a Positive Atmosphere to Encourage Parental Involvement

'What is the difference between a professional learning community and a school learning community? A professional learning community emphasises the teamwork of head teachers, teachers, and staff to identify school goals, improve curriculum and instruction, reduce teachers' isolation, assess student progress, and increase the effectiveness of school programmes. Professional teamwork is important and can greatly improve teaching, instruction, and professional relationships in schools, but falls short of producing a true community of learners. In contrast, a school learning community includes educators, students, parents, and community partners who work together to improve the school and enhance the students' learning opportunities.'

(Joyce L. Epstein & Karen Clark Salinas, 2004)

If the partnership between the school, the family and the community is to grow strong and productive, in the interests of the pupil, it is important to look at and understand the rights and responsibilities of the parents or carers.

Parents' Rights

- To be involved in the education of their child and the life of the school their child attends.

- To have any query or problem dealt with promptly and confidentially.

- That their child is taught equally regardless of ability or gender in accordance with the National Curriculum and in a safe and caring environment.

- To be informed of any academic or behavioural problems in accordance with school procedures.

- The right of their child not to be bullied.

Parents' Responsibilities

- To see that their child attends school regularly and on time.

- To ensure that their child respects and co-operates with teachers, ancillary staff and pupils.

- To see that their child upholds the rules of the school.

- To encourage their child to work hard, complete homework and participate in extra curricular activities.

- To support the school's ethos and its curriculum teaching and discipline policy.

In order to encourage the pupil to make more positive choices it is important that the parents/carers are encouraged to have an active role in the whole process of the behaviour programme. For some parents this can be very intimidating. They might have had negative experiences while at school. Schools and teachers can appear to be unfriendly and uninviting. Their own preconceived ideas of school and teachers can be reinforced by the child's negative school history to date. The only communication for many is negative: phone calls, letters, reports, meetings, telling them about their disruptive child. We must realise and understand that, for some parents, school is a very fearsome place. For schools to turn this around we must look at how we communicate with carers. As a starting point we could ask the following question: What steps could we take to make all parents/carers feel more comfortable in working co-operatively with the school?

In building more positive working relationships and partnerships with parents, as well as the discussion about the programme, the following general points should be considered:

The first point of communication between the school and the carer is the school's main entrance. Is it well signposted so that carers don't have difficulty finding their way to reception? Is it welcoming and informative? Are the school signs and information written in positive language? For example, a sign saying that all visitors should report to the front office can be changed to become more positive and friendly: 'Welcome to … School. Please go to the front office where someone will assist you.' Make the entrance foyer a welcoming place for carers. Displays of pupils' artwork, flowers and information booklets create a better and more positive atmosphere.

Is there a need to review the quality and appearance of written school-home communication? Far too often there can be an overload of wordy information with no clear style of presentation. This can cause confusion for carers and in some cases switch them off from developing a good relationship with the school. It makes them feel inferior and inadequate. All written correspondence to carers should be clear, concise, accurate, succinct and colourful, and should consider style and language.

- Clear: consider the font you are using, font size, colour of paper and print. Look at the layout of the page and leave some blank spaces to group ideas and issues together.

- Concise: use plain language with short sentences or bullet points.

- Accurate: make sure you get all the facts right and give the information that is needed.

- Succinct: avoid cluttering up with too much detail that the reader doesn't need to know.

- Colourful: make use of pictures and illustrations that can add to or improve the message you are trying to convey.

- Style and language: do not use jargon, use an informal style and language that is less off-putting for some carers. This is an important aspect of creating a sense of partnership between the school and the home.

Do signatures on letters to carers contain forenames? The simple use of a forename can make the contact more personalised to the carer and help create a greater bond between the school and the home. As a school do we contact carers for positive as well as negative reasons? The old saying that a small amount of praise goes a long way was never more appropriate than it is in today's schools. If the carer is only receiving negative comments and complaints from the school then there is no possibility of forming a relationship that would benefit the pupil. Look for something positive to report on that will give the carer hope, encouragement, and strength from a working partnership.

Inter-Agency Collaboration

Another major area that would encourage positive communication is the setting up of inter-agency collaboration with services that share an interest in children and their families. Examples of those with whom collaboration is possible include education welfare workers, education psychology service, health workers, adult education workers, police, social services, youth workers, travellers' service, English as another language support teachers, outreach support teachers and voluntary sector workers. When I was first appointed as SENCO I was amazed at the number of services, external to the school provision, that could be involved with pupils. It was also apparent that most of these services worked in isolation and did not have the opportunity to share information. This meant that at times there was duplication and even a confusion of strategies being used with the pupil. To help to overcome this dilemma an inter-agency meeting was suggested.

> 'We found that teachers can play an important part in encouraging parents to engage with services and if delivered in schools they can further build the home-school partnership that is so important in helping children to succeed.'

> (Judy Hutchings & Tracey Bywater, 2007)

The multi-agency meeting gives an opportunity for all agencies to discuss the best way forward for each individual pupil. The sharing of information, and agreeing future targets and strategies, ensures that limited resources are not duplicated but are maximised for the benefit of the pupil. When first introduced these meetings were held on a termly basis but such was their positive impact they soon were held twice a term.

Another important aspect of these meetings is that, if it is felt to be appropriate and beneficial, carers can be invited to attend. For some carers this is possibly the first time they can identify a co-ordinated approach from all the agencies involved with their child. If a carer is not present then the agreed plan of strategies and targets is communicated by the agency or service that the meeting deems most appropriate.

> 'There are many reasons for developing school, family, and community relationship. The main reason to create such partnerships is to help all youngsters succeed in school and in later life.'

> (Joyce Epstein, 2001)

Working with Parents whose Child is on the Choice Programme

When a child has been accepted for a place on the programme the carer must be informed. The pupil can only access the programme if both the carer and the child agree to the conditions and targets set by the programme.

My suggestion is that before the parent/pupil meeting a member of staff contacts the carer to arrange an informal chat to explain the programme and its objectives. Before this informal contact remember to speak to the pupil regarding contact with the carer, explaining that this is a positive contact and that the school, the pupil, and the parent, will all be working together in order to make education a more positive experience for the pupil. Pupil and parent must both agree to join the programme.

The first meeting with the carer could be arranged at the carer's home. The carer will be more at ease and receptive in friendly, familiar surroundings and it also shows the school as proactive and caring. The teacher in charge of the programme should make this visit and should be accompanied by another teacher, classroom assistant or behaviour assistant. This second adult should know the child and be able to make a contribution to the meeting. Since the second adult will be involved with the programme in the school they also get the opportunity to meet with the parents before the start of the programme. This again reinforces the link between the school and the home. During this meeting it is important to stress that the teachers and carers are partners and have to work together for the benefit of the child. The teachers and carers must have open communication and dialogue while the pupil is on the programme. At this time the teacher can explain the purpose of the programme and the benefits that are hoped to be achieved. The teacher must emphasise that this is not a punishment but is a learning programme. If progress is to be made there must be a three-way partnership and agreement between the school, the pupil and the carer.

A second, formal meeting with the carer is held in the school a few days prior to the pupil entering the programme. At this meeting, which is attended by the carer, the pupil, and a programme teacher, a formal contract is signed by all three that outlines agreed targets. See page 53 for the Parent/Pupil Meeting record sheet. These are not general whole-school targets but are specific to the programme and could include the following:

- Arrive on time.

- Wear a school uniform.

- Have a schoolbag, pencil and pen.

- Show respect to other pupils on the programme.

- Show respect to programme staff.

- Do your best to complete all work.

These targets can be tailored to meet the individual needs of a pupil.

During the programme the teacher should give a daily progress report to the carer by a quick phone call at the end of each school day highlighting any positive improvements made by the pupil. This gives the carer opportunities to praise and reinforce how the pupil is progressing and it becomes a motivational factor for both the pupil and the carer. The Daily Review information sheet (page 81) can also be used to involve the parents in reviewing progress. When the pupil is on the programme the carer should be encouraged to visit the school and either observe or participate in some of the activities. It is also important that the carer is available to go to the school if a negative situation arises. This gives the carer, teacher and pupil an opportunity to quickly discuss what caused the incident and how to go forward from it, while at the same time reinforcing the positive partnership between the school and the home.

The Target Diary

At the end of the programme the teacher, carer and pupil meet in order to discuss future progress. The pupil will be returning to mainstream class aided and supported by a target diary and programme teachers. All pupils will be required to carry a target diary. This diary will have three targets that have been agreed between the programme teacher and the pupil. The targets are designed to help the pupil to maximise their time in the class and to minimise any negative behaviour. At the end of the school day the pupil reports to the programme teacher and the target diary is assessed. During the daily assessment it is important that the pupil's positive achievements are reinforced and that any negative behaviours are discussed and used for future target setting. It is also important that the pupil has an opportunity for self-evaluation and is encouraged to comment on the positive aspects of his behaviour, how he reached his targets for that day and how he will maintain future progress.

In order to inform parents about the pupil's progress the target diary is taken home each day and signed by a parent. After each week's completion of the target diary the programme teacher and the pupil decide whether the pupil should go off the diary or continue for another week.

It should be noted that for some pupils the target diary becomes an essential part of their school life. It becomes their excuse, their prop, for future behaviour in school. It helps to remove peer pressure and gives the pupil a legitimate excuse for not getting involved in situations and behaviours that could result in further conflict with teachers, by allowing the pupil to say to their peers that they cannot get involved because they are being monitored by the diary. When, in the future, the pupil has gained enough confidence to say, 'I have changed because I wanted to change,' they can then cope without the aid of the diary.

Chapter 5

The Choice Programme

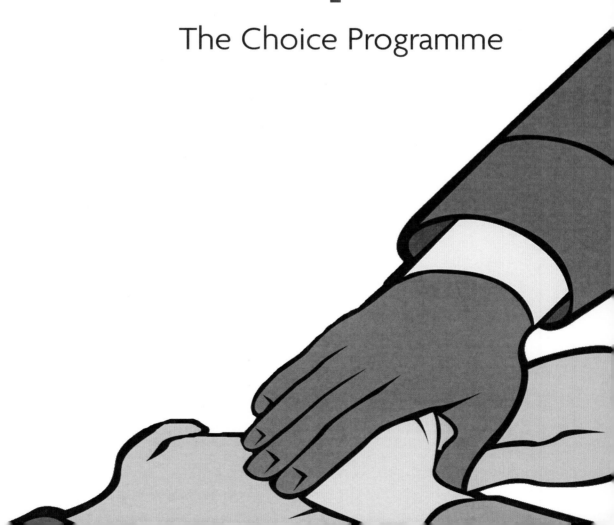

Chapter 5 The Choice Programme

Introduction

Before looking at the programme activities it is worth reflecting on the fact that the programme was developed in order that pupils could learn management and coping skills that would enable them to return to their mainstream classes with the skills necessary for survival in the classroom environment. During the journey through Choice both you as the facilitator and the pupil will experience many highs as well as low points. At times it will feel that you are going three steps backwards in order to take two steps forwards. Skills learning can be a slow and painful process for both the facilitator and the pupil. It is like a real life game of snakes and ladders. The skilful facilitator will guide the pupil up the ladders and then consolidate the gains on the horizontal stretch, being ever vigilant for the snake that would unravel all the previous good work.

The programme as a one-week intensive programme will give maximum benefit to the pupil, while at the same time keeping the withdrawal from mainstream class to a minimum. As previously mentioned, the programme works best with a group of six to eight pupils who have been identified as having difficulty with behaviour within the classroom setting. It is of vital importance that the pupil receives out of class support during the weeks after the one-week programme. Support for the pupil on entry back into mainstream class will include:

- target setting by the programme staff and the individual pupil
- target diary to be completed by all staff during the initial period of return or as long as it is needed
- target diary to be monitored by the programme staff on a daily basis
- at least two periods per week when the pupil and a staff member from the programme can meet to discuss difficulties, problems and choices made by the pupil in the mainstream class
- target diary to be signed and monitored on a daily basis by the parent
- the target diary is also used by the pupil as a daily self-evaluation on how she has worked towards her targets and what effect this has had on her school day
- review meeting to be arranged with the pupil, year head, programme staff member and parent, after one full week back in class, in order to discuss improvements and the way forward.

A timetable for the one-week programme should emphasise behavioural skills development but should also develop other aspects of school work:

- Aspects of literacy and numeracy.
- Project work.
- Behavioural skills.
- Reviews.

Background Music

It is important that during the programme pupils are given time to silently think. Silent reading or drawing, with soft background music, is conducive to this. From my own experience and experimentation not only on the programme but during classroom teaching, I have found that music by Mozart, especially woodwind, has a very positive and calming effect. Examples of this are Mozart's Serenade for 13 Wood Instruments, Flute and Harp Concerto, Bassoon Concerto, Oboe Concerto, Clarinet Concerto, and Quintet for Clarinet, Basset-horn and String Trio. Other examples of music that are equally effective are Vivaldi's 'The Four Seasons' Wind Concerto and Famous Concerti for Two Trumpets, Oboe, Violins, Cello and Mandolins; and Darius Milhaud's Music for Wood Instruments.

Pre-Programme Testing

During the initial stages of the programme all pupils should be diagnostically tested in order that literacy and numeracy levels can be obtained. An initial learning problem that has remained undiagnosed may be the root cause for the indiscipline in class. If this is the case then on completion of the programme the pupil's needs will have to be met through the school special needs department.

Project Work

Freestanding project work is of vital importance for the success of the programme. The programme's staff guide the standard of presentation and work. The display of these projects is of vital importance in developing the pupils' self-esteem. For many of these pupils this will be the first time that they have completed a piece of work and received recognition for their work.

Reviewing Progress

Reviews are daily and at the end of the programme, and are important not only to give feedback to the pupil but also to plan how to cope with similar situations that might arise in the future. In order that daily reviews can be carried out, the pupils have to fill in daily review information sheets towards the end of the day. At the end of each day the programme staff complete the same sheet. Both the pupil and the staff review sheets are discussed and this gives staff and pupils the opportunity to look at differences in assessment and therefore a starting point for future change.

The programme is most effective when it is offered as a five-day course with a group of six to eight pupils. In some schools, due to timetabling or staffing difficulties, the five-day programme may not be possible, but the materials can be used either with individual pupils or with groups of pupils on designated periods either daily or weekly. With this in mind I have set out a five-day timetable. Day one of the programme is set out in detail while the rest of the week is set out under the headings: literacy, numeracy, individual work skills and behavioural skills. This allows the facilitator a choice of activities for behavioural skills that appear more relevant to the group. It also allows a facilitator who is working with either an individual or group not using the five-day programme to select activities under the required behavioural skill category.

The format is to be seen as a loose structure to alter and amend as necessary and not as a straitjacket of prescriptive instructions.

Five-Day Timetable

Day One

Registration

Length of time: 10 minutes.

During this first registration pupils along with their parent/carer arrive and are greeted with a cup of tea. The parents are asked to stay, if possible, for the first hour of the programme. During the rest of the week parents are encouraged to 'drop in' whenever possible as well as keeping up to date by telephone and daily reports.

Initial Session

General introduction, Roundabout of Choice 1 and Roundabout of Choice 2.

Length of time: 40-60 minutes.

Session 1

Behavioural audit, Your Strengths.

Length of time: 40 minutes.

The length of time for the behavioural audit activities are a guide and should not be seen as a rigid restraint. Depending on the interaction of the group and the work that is being achieved the facilitator should use discretion on the ending of a session.

Mid-Morning Break

Length of time: 10 minutes.

During this first break it is explained to pupils that tea and biscuits are provided but the pupils must clean up after the break and before the start of the next session. Having responsibility for their own environment introduces pupils to having responsibility for other aspects of their lives. During the programme pupils should also clean the room at the end of the day so that it is ready for a new start the next day. Visitors to the programme often commented on the sight of 14 and 15-year-old boys vacuuming and polishing at the end of the day. The boys found this very acceptable, indeed therapeutic, it was their area and they were responsible for looking after it and besides nobody wants to start a new day in an untidy room. It is important that the facilitator is part of the clean-up team and indeed, at the start of the week, leads by example.

Session 2

Silent reading.

Length of time: 15 minutes.

Pupils are introduced to silent reading and should be given an opportunity to pick a book or books that will interest them. After each behavioural skills activity pupils will be given five minutes to silently read, which also gives them thinking time to consider the implications, consequences and outcomes relating to them from the previous session.

Session 3

Behavioural audit, Things I Did in Class that Got Me into Trouble.

Length of time: 40 minutes.

Session 4

Silent reading.

Length of time: 5 minutes.

Session 5

Behavioural audit, Frequent Situations.

Length of time: 40 minutes.

Session 6

Behavioural audit, The Train Journey.

Length of time: 40 minutes.

Lunchtime

This is a longer break than during the rest of the week and gives the facilitator an opportunity to show pupils, and explain to them, the structure of lunchtime. Desks have to be moved together to form an eating area. During lunch the facilitator should eat with the pupils in order to strengthen relationships and help pupils to develop better social skills. It is explained to pupils that prior to the start of the afternoon session it is the pupils' responsibility to clean the room and rearrange the desks.

Session 7

Behavioural audit, Aliens.

Length of time: 40 minutes.

Session 8

Silent reading.

Length of time: 5 minutes.

Session 9

Behavioural audit, Consequences.

Length of time: 40 minutes.

Session 10

Numeracy.

Length of time: 30 minutes.

Since this is the first numeracy lesson it can be used for assessment. With younger pupils I have used Vernon's and NfER tests and with all age groups the Integrated Learning Systems (http://atschool.eduweb.co.uk/MBAKER/material/ils.html), 'Successmaker'. The advantage of the computerised system is that it not only diagnoses problem areas but will provide an individualised learning programme for the pupil to follow. Another advantage is that pupils are more motivated to work on computers.

Session 11

Daily review.

Length of time: 10 minutes.

The review sheet can be completed by a member of staff and the pupil individually and the results can be compared or completed together. The review should be taken home to keep parents involved.

The Initial Session

Activities

General introduction and rules of the programme.

Roundabout of Choice 1 and 2.

Facilitator Notes

General

This period of the programme is vital if pupils are to move forward and develop. The session is subdivided into three sections, general introduction, Roundabout of Choice 1 and Roundabout of Choice 2. This will take an hour to cover. The session sets boundaries that will allow both pupils and staff the opportunity during the remainder of the programme to develop relationships and work in an atmosphere of trust, understanding, and openness. During this initial session it is important that the pupil learns and understands the rules, boundaries and perimeters for the rest of the programme. It is only when both pupils and staff know and understand what is acceptable and what is expected during the rest of the programme that progress can be made. During the programme pupils will work on behavioural activities that mostly comply to the format of individual response followed by group discussion. During the individual response section of the activity pupils should sit at an individual desk and work independently and when this is finished should move into a more relaxed area for the group discussion. This could be chairs placed at the back of the room in either a circular or semi-circular formation. During these group discussions simple rules should be observed:

- Only one person to talk at any one time.
- Respect the opinion of others.

Rules

Rules for pupils on the Choice Programme should be clear and kept to a minimum. The rules of the programme should concentrate on:

- not hurting anyone physically or emotionally
- not wasting your or others' time
- not damaging property
- not interrupting
- not covering up the truth.

All rules should be centered on respect:

- for people
- for property
- for time.

Most important is respect for yourself.

The Roundabout of Choice 1 and 2

A copy of the Roundabout of Choice 1 is given to each pupil. The whole concept is that the pupil is out of class and is on a roundabout that is graphically shown. As the facilitator you can explain the meaning of choice on a roundabout. If you use the example of a car and a driver approaching a large roundabout, where the driver can make choices about the road he can take to exit the roundabout, then the pupils can visualise what is happening. The driver will look for signs and directions that will show him the direction he needs to take. The diagram shows the pupils that they have approached a roundabout and with the right direction they can successfully go round the roundabout and return to mainstream class. The Roundabout of Choice 2 is then given to each individual pupil and is symbolic of where the pupil is at this point in her education. The emphasis during this session is to give the pupil information on the education system and what implications this will have for their future. The Code of Practice and its implications are explained and discussed. The position of schools and their duty of education to pupils is explained and discussed. Alternative forms of education are discussed and explained. The provision for stage four and five education is explained along with possible consequences for future employment. The main emphasis is that the pupil should make the decision to go round the roundabout and back into school.

This initial session brings the pupil, for the first time in the programme, to the concept of choice and how choice is always related to consequences.

In order for the pupil to make choices and decisions it is important that the pupil has the correct information to make informed choices or decisions.

The Behavioural Audit

Activities

Your Strengths.

Things I Did in Class that Got Me into Trouble.

Frequent Situations.

The Train Journey.

Aliens.

Consequences.

Facilitator Notes

General

During the behavioural audit pupils are given an opportunity to examine behaviours that have resulted in their being removed from the mainstream class. These activities give the pupils an opportunity not only to examine past situations but also to look at who has responsibility for this behaviour, to examine the outcomes that have resulted from it and to look at all those on whom it has had an effect. It gives the pupils the opportunity to make an inventory of past behaviour, the present and to start the process of planning for the future. It gives the pupils the opportunity to accept ownership and to become empowered in regard to their future behaviour. It also allows the pupils the opportunity to realise that they do not exist in isolation and that the outcome of their negative behaviour has an effect on a very wide circle of people.

During this and all future sessions it is important that it is the inappropriate behaviours that are discussed and criticised and not the pupils.

There are bad behaviours but not bad pupils.

Your Strengths

This activity is to enable the pupil to look at what he is good at doing. Focus on the positive and discuss how, during the programme, pupils will develop skills and strategies that will enable them to turn negatives and weaknesses into strengths. It is important at this early stage that the pupil can recognise that he has strengths but that too often we concentrate on the weaknesses. We can't all be good at everything and it is useful if the facilitator completes the questionnaire and shares the results with the group talking about the highlighted weaknesses and how if you know your weaknesses you can plan to overcome them.

Things I Did in Class that Got Me into Trouble

For many pupils this is a reality check. It is the first time that they have to think about how they have reacted in the classroom situation and at the same time come to the realisation that teachers and other pupils are all affected by disruptive behaviour. The last section of this activity can bring in a bit of humour if we look at all the ways, positive, negative and ridiculous, that will get us noticed and the outcomes for the pupil if these happen.

Frequent Situations

During this activity, which can be either written or oral, discuss as a group each situation. Look at the outcome, for the pupil and others involved, and consider, in hindsight, how the pupil could have better managed the situation and obtained a more positive outcome. This leads into the next activity that is centred in pupil choice.

The Train Journey

After giving pupils a copy of the activity, the facilitator can talk about a local train journey familiar to the pupils. During this the facilitator can talk about stations that the train stops at along the way and how everyone getting on the train at the start of its journey does not stay on until the train stops at the last station. People disembark from the train at stations of their choice along the route. The facilitator likens the train journey to conflict situations encountered by the pupils in school. Get the pupils to share individual conflict situations with the group and discuss how the pupil could have removed herself from the situation before she reached the last station.

Aliens

It is important that it is the pupil who lists what they think is unacceptable or strange behaviour shown or acted by them. This can be a humorous activity and very often the individual and group will find some of their past behaviours funny and embarrassing to look at now. The facilitator must be very vigilant during this activity and not allow the situation to develop into one of conflict. If the comments from the group about another individual's past behaviour start getting out of hand the facilitator must stop the activity and remind the group about the programme rules concerning respect and not hurting anyone.

Consequences

For the first time the pupil is introduced to the concept of consequences. Every action and decision they make has an outcome that can either be positive or negative for them. If they had realised what the outcome could be would they have continued with that action or would they have acted differently? During this activity the facilitator leads a group discussion using the four examples as a lead in to discussing what the pupils could have changed that would have kept them off the programme. If time is available they could discuss a real situation that they have been involved in.

The Roundabout of Choice 1

Out of
Mainstream Class

The 'Choice'
Programme

Out of
Mainstream School

Return to Mainstream Class
with Target Setting

The Roundabout of Choice 2

A small number of pupils who cannot behave in class.

| Our School | → The 'Choice' Programme → | Suspension /Expulsion |

Most of the pupils on the programme return to mainstream class.

Our School

The 'Choice' Programme

Suspension /Expulsion

Most pupils behave, do reasonably well and improve their reading, writing, numeracy and social skills.

Other Education Provision

Limited Curriculum Development

At 16

Examination results determine.

Go on in education.
Go on in skills training.
Get a job.

} Personal Choice

Future Looks Good

At 16

Limited examination success.

Limited choices.

Limited employment opportunities.

Future Looks?

Your Strengths

What are your strengths?
If you know what your strengths and weaknesses are, this can help you to make decisions about your future.

The self-assessment chart will help you to identify your strengths.
On the chart assess your strengths on a five-point scale by putting a circle around the appropriate number. Be honest. Do not try to cover up your weaknesses and do not be modest about your strengths.

1. Very weak.
2. Weak.
3. Average.
4. Good.
5. Very good.

Strengths Survey

Working in a group.	1	2	3	4	5
Working on my own.	1	2	3	4	5
Sitting at my desk.	1	2	3	4	5
Being patient.	1	2	3	4	5
Working quietly.	1	2	3	4	5
Making plans.	1	2	3	4	5
Accepting discipline.	1	2	3	4	5
Listening.	1	2	3	4	5
Keeping calm.	1	2	3	4	5
Following instructions.	1	2	3	4	5
Reading quietly.	1	2	3	4	5
Reading out loud.	1	2	3	4	5
Reading and studying.	1	2	3	4	5
Writing.	1	2	3	4	5
Working with numbers.	1	2	3	4	5
Working with hands.	1	2	3	4	5
Using tools and machinery.	1	2	3	4	5

Things I Did in Class that Got Me into Trouble

List five examples:

1.

2.

3.

4.

5.

In class it annoys me when:

Things that annoy teachers in class:

How to get noticed in a classroom:

Positive ways:

Negative ways:

Ridiculous ways:

Frequent Situations

Let us consider the most frequent situations that lead us into behavioural problems.

In the grid below identify where and with whom these situations arise.
Give an honest account of what usually happens to get you into trouble.

Where?	Who?	What happened?

The Train Journey

A conflict situation is like a train journey.

Whenever you get on a train you do not have to stay on until you reach the last station. There are many stations along the journey. The decision to get off is yours. It is your choice.

A conflict situation in school is like the train journey. The start of the conflict is the first station on the journey. The last station is the one where you are put out of class, become suspended or maybe even expelled.

Did you have to stay on until the last station?

Could you have got off at an earlier station?

Consider your last major conflict situation in school.

What happened at the first station?

What happened at the last station?

Can you find and describe other stations along the journey where you might have got off this train?

What could you have done at these stations?

Aliens

Beings on an alien planet have decided to study humans. For their study they have selected our school. In secret they are watching the behaviour of pupils in the classroom, on the corridors, in the playground and in the canteen. They have written and categorised what they have observed as either 'acceptable' or 'strange'.

Fill in the form below on how you think they would have seen your behaviour. If you have time you could use the back of the sheet to draw some of the strange behaviour.

Acceptable Behaviour	Strange Behaviour

Consequences

At times we do things without fully thinking out what could eventually happen.
There are times when we act without stopping to think first.
If we had stopped to think then we might have made different choices, made different decisions, acted differently.
What are the consequences or outcomes of the following situations?

1. I can't be bothered doing any homework tonight. I'm going to go out with my friends instead.
2. Since it's my first day as a Year 8 pupil in a new secondary school I'm going to pick a fight with the biggest Year 12 to prove that I'm not afraid of anyone.
3. I've been given a GCSE project to do. It has to be handed in to the teacher in three weeks' time. I'll leave it until the night before.
4. A substitute teacher is taking our class so I'm going to 'mess about' since the teacher won't know who I am.

Can you identify any situations you have been involved with that could have had a different outcome?

Situation	What Happened?	A Choice I Could Have Made

Daily Review

Pupil and Staff Appraisal Sheet

Name ....

Date ....

Staff member ....

Target 1 ....

Target 2 ....

Target 3 ....

The things that worked well today:

The main strength was:

The things that didn't work well:

The main weakness was:

Points to be considered for tomorrow including the original targets:

Signed by: ....

Pupil: ....

Teacher: ....

Parent/Carer: ....

The Rest of the Programme (Days Two-Five)

The structure for the remaining four days of a five-day programme is provided, though in less detail than for Day One. Each group will develop a unique pattern of work and staff can choose activities from the sections to suit their group.

- Concentration.
- Listening.
- Communication.
- Sitting Skills.
- Co-Operation.
- Individual Work Skills – Project Work.

Day Two

Registration

This is a ten minute period during which the pupils and facilitator start the day in an informal and relaxed way with a cup of tea. Daily reviews are checked for parental signatures and telephone calls are made to parents if any pupils are absent.

Session 1

Behavioural skills activity, Communication.

Length of time: 40 minutes.

The lengths of time for the behavioural skills activities are a guide and should not be seen as a rigid restraint. Depending on the interaction of the group and the work that is being achieved the facilitator should use discretion on the ending of a session.

Session 2

Silent reading.

Length of time: 5 minutes.

Session 3

Behavioural skills activity, Sitting Skills.

Length of time: 40 minutes.

Session 4

Silent reading.

Length of time: 5 minutes.

Session 5

Literacy.

Length of time: 30 minutes.

Since this is the first literacy lesson it can be used for assessment. With younger pupils I have used Suffolk and NfER tests and with all age groups the Integrated Learning Systems, 'Successmaker'. The advantage of the computerised system is that it not only diagnoses problem areas but will provide an individualised learning programme for the pupil to follow such as 'Reading Awareness' and 'Spelling'. Another advantage is that pupils are more motivated to work on computers.

Mid-Morning Break

This usually lasts for ten minutes and is informal and relaxed. The pupils use the area of the room that is used for group discussion and where chairs are arranged in a semicircular or circular fashion. During the morning break and later at lunchtime I introduce pupils to the board game 'draughts'. This became so popular with the pupils that subject and form teachers regularly appeared during their breaks to play against the pupils. This gave both the pupils and teachers an opportunity to form positive relationships outside the classroom context and for the pupils to develop social skills.

Session 6

Behavioural skills activity, Concentration.

Length of time: 40 minutes.

Session 7

Silent reading.

Length of time: 5 minutes.

Session 8

Behavioural skills activity, Listening.

Length of time: 40 minutes.

Session 9

Silent reading.

Length of time: 5 minutes.

Lunchtime

During lunchtime pupils either bring their own lunches or school dinners are ordered and delivered free of charge to the programme room. Draughts, dominoes and card games are provided and the atmosphere should be informal and relaxed. After the lunch break pupils should be encouraged to clean up the room in preparation for the afternoon session.

Session 10

Individual Work Skills.

For the remainder of the afternoon pupils should be introduced to individual work skills – project work.

Session 11

Daily review.

Pupil and facilitator daily review of Day Two.

Day Three

Registration

Length of time: 10 minutes.

Session 1

Behavioural skills activity, Co-Operation.

Length of time: 40 minutes.

Session 2

Silent reading.

Length of time: 5 minutes.

Session 3

Individual Work Skills – project work continued.

Length of time: 45 minutes.

Session 4

Literacy.

Length of time: 30 minutes.

During this session I suggest that the pupils' subject teacher sends the work being done by the rest of the class. This gives the facilitator an opportunity to work with the pupil and assess any difficulties. It also allows the pupil to keep in contact with class work.

Mid-Morning Break

Length of time: 10 minutes.

Session 5

Behavioural skills activity, Communication.

Length of time: 40 minutes.

Session 6

Silent reading.

Length of time: 5 minutes.

Session 7

Behavioural skills activity, Co-Operation.

Length of time: 40 minutes.

Session 8

Silent reading.

Length of time: 5 minutes.

Lunchtime

Session 9

Numeracy, work from subject teacher.

Length of time: 30 minutes.

Session 10

Behavioural skills activity, Communication.

Length of time: 40 minutes.

Session 11

Individual Work Skills – projects continued.

Length of time: 40 minutes.

Session 12

Daily review.

Day Four

Registration

Length of time: 10 minutes.

Session 1

Individual Work Skills – projects continued.

Length of time: 45 minutes.

Session 2

Numeracy, work from subject teacher.

Length of time: 30 minutes.

Session 3

Behavioural skills activity, Co-Operation.

Length of time: 40 minutes.

Session 4

Silent reading.

Length of time: 5 minutes.

Mid-Morning Break

Length of time: 10 minutes.

Session 5

Behavioural skills activity, Communication.

Length of time: 40 minutes.

Session 6

Silent reading.

Length of time: 5 minutes.

Lunchtime

Session 8

Literacy, work from subject teacher.

Length of time: 30 minutes.

Session 9

Behavioural skills activity, Co-Operation.

Length of time: 40 minutes.

Session 10

Individual Work Skills – projects continued.

Length of time: 40 minutes.

Session 11

Daily reviews.

Day Five

Registration

Session 1

Behavioural skills activity, Sitting Skills.

Length of time: 40 minutes.

Session 2

Silent reading.

Length of time: 5 minutes.

Session 3

Behavioural skills activity, Concentration.

Length of time: 40 minutes.

Session 4

Silent reading.

Length of time: 5 minutes.

Session 5

Behavioural skills activity, Co-Operation.

Length of time: 40 minutes.

Mid-Morning Break

Length of time: 10 minutes.

Session 6

Individual Work Skills – final project work.

Length of time: 50 minutes.

During this session projects are finalised and displayed.

Lunchtime

Session 7

The final session.

Evaluation, Celebration and Graduation, and Programme Review Meeting.

Behavioural Skills Activities

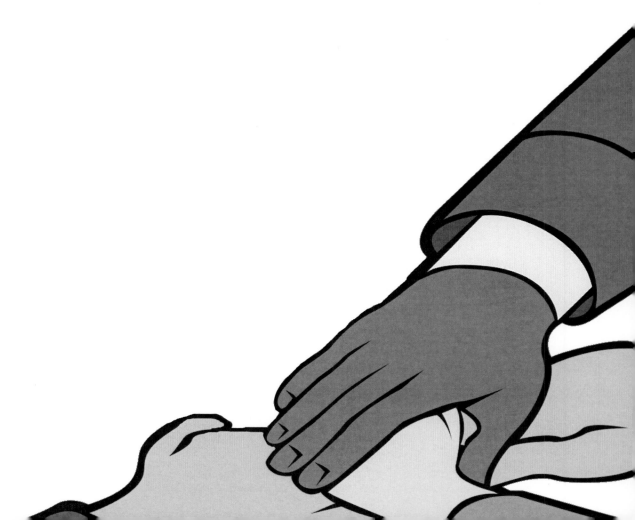

Behavioural Skills Activities

Activities

Concentration Skills.

Listening Skills.

Communication Skills.

Sitting Skills.

Co-Operation.

Individual Work Skills.

Facilitator Notes

General

The above behavioural skills activities can be used in any order depending on the specific needs of the pupil or the direction of the teacher. This gives the facilitator an opportunity to design a programme tailored to meet the needs of the individual pupil or group of pupils who are currently on the course. The main point is that the activity page is the starting point for future discussion either with a group of pupils or with an individual pupil. Discussion groups should be strictly regulated and should comply with agreed group rules. I would suggest that pupils initially sit in a classroom formation with each pupil sitting at an individual desk and working independently. After the initial material has been completed the pupils should then move into a more informal, relaxed position. Suggestions for this are either a circular or semi-circular formation. At this stage the discussion is led by the facilitator based on pupil responses from the initial starting activity.

The main and most important rule for these activities is the right to speech. When someone in the group is talking nobody is allowed to interrupt.

These sessions will normally last for 30 minutes and should be followed by a 5- or 10-minute period of silent reflection. Silent reading is a good strategy for silent reflection.

Concentration Skills

Facilitator Notes

General

The objective of these activities is to give pupils the skills necessary to work independently in a classroom setting.

Still Life Drawing

Pupils are seated around the object and using pencil only they are asked to make an interpretative drawing. A good object is a colourful bunch of flowers. The task lasts for ten minutes during which the pupils must work silently in order that they do not break the concentration of others. Working quietly is a skill that can be learned and developed. It is a high level skill and this activity can be repeated on a daily basis with the time increasing by two or three minutes each day. Pupils must be motivated and see an end product, therefore at the end of the activity pupils frame their favourite drawings and mount an art exhibition.

Memory Test

Pupils are shown a simple line drawing for approximately two minutes. They are then informed that they will be asked a series of questions on the drawing that will test their powers of concentration. They are given another two minutes in order to further study the drawing.

This activity is designed to develop not only concentration and memory skills but independent silent study skills. Pupils are asked a series of questions about the drawing.

Verbal Descriptive Exercise

During this activity pupils are given a copy of the same drawing and asked to colour it in.

When pupils have finished colouring in they are asked to describe, in detail, their colours to the other pupils. Each pupil is given approximately five minutes to describe their picture and its colours. They will describe, for example, the colour of the carriage, the colour of the horse and the colour of the hats that are worn by the various people.

The other pupils will try to interpret this description onto a photocopy of the original drawing. When all pupils have explained their drawings and copies have been made they are displayed in sets with the original on top and the copies underneath.

The next stage of this activity is a group discussion. Which group replicates and correlates best with the original? Can successful correlation be just down to oral descriptive skills or do other external factors play important roles, for example, pupil disruptions?

It can be a useful teaching point to have a prearranged interruption during the exercise. This could be two teachers or classroom assistants having a conversation when one of the pupils is describing their drawing. When the finished drawings are displayed it is evident when the disruption took place. There is a low correlation between the original and the rest of the group. This gives the facilitator an opportunity to emphasise that being disruptive in class has a negative effect on the learning of others.

During the initial colouring in this is again developing independent silent study skills.

Extension Work

Interesting ideas can be developed round concepts such as Tony Buzan's 'mind-maps', mnemonics and world memory championships. Activities such as:

- The memory tray, which has a number of objects which are shown to the group for a short period and then the tray is covered. The task is to then remember the objects.

The task can be made more difficult by increasing the number of objects, and/or increasing the length of time between the viewing and the recalling.

- I went to market. The group sit and the first person says, 'I went to market and bought a pig.' The second person adds, 'I went to market and bought a pig and a packet of crisps,' and so on round the group for as long as people can recall the items.

- Pelmanism, sometimes called Memory, Shinkei-suijoku or Pairs. This is a card game of say ten pairs. The 20 cards are laid face down and the object is to match cards.

Each person can only turn over two cards to make a match. If they don't match, the cards are returned to their original face down position. The game can be made more difficult by increasing the number of cards.

Mnemonics

The pupils can be introduced to the technique of using visual prompts to aid memory and concentration. Most of the world memory champions use this technique. Though YouTube should be used with caution, there are some interesting explanations of using visual clues by people such as world champion Andi Bell.

Concentration Skills

Memory Test

Show the pupils the simple line drawing for approximately 2-3 minutes.
Tell them that they will be asked a series of questions on the drawing that will test their powers of concentration. Then give them another two minutes in order to further study the drawing. After removing the drawing ask or give the pupils the following questions:

1. How many aeroplanes are hanging from the ceiling?
2. How many children are there?
3. How many children have black hair?
4. How many children are sitting at the table?
5. How many pencils are on the table?
6. How many girls are sitting at the table?
7. How many children are drawing?
8. What are in the tub on the table?
9. How many children have white jumpers?
10. What is the boy with black hair doing?
11. What picture is shown in the open book?
12. What year is shown in the picture?

Verbal Descriptive Exercise

Colour in this drawing. When you have finished colouring, describe, in detail, your colours to the other pupils. They will try to interpret this description onto a photocopy of your original drawing.

Listening Skills

Activities

When the Teacher is Talking.

The Level of Noise in a Classroom.

Extension Work.

Facilitator Notes

General

These activities are designed to get the pupil thinking about appropriate and inappropriate times to talk during a lesson.

When the Teacher is Talking

After the pupil has completed the activity page, 'When the Teacher is Talking', the facilitator should lead the discussion on when you can and when you cannot talk in class. It is important that the pupils are made aware that disruptive talking is affecting the rights of others. Other pupils have a right to learn and teachers have a right to be able to teach. It should be stressed to these pupils that we do not exist in isolation and that all our actions have an impact on others. Tap into their feelings and emotions. What is their reaction when someone disrupts them from doing a task or project they are interested in? How do they feel in that situation? Get them to transfer these feelings and emotions to how others feel, teachers and pupils, when their constant disruptive talking causes concern and stress for others.

It is also important during these activities to discuss body language and recognise warning signs and expressions from others. The look the teacher gives you that sends out a clear message. Can these pupils recognise these important danger signs?

Level of Noise in a Classroom

This is best done as a brainstorming activity with a group of six to eight pupils. Before starting the activity the facilitator should lay down ground rules in order that each individual pupil gets a chance to speak:

- respect the rights of others to have their opinion heard:
- do not interrupt when someone is talking, wait your turn.

The activity allows the pupils to consider appropriate times for talking during the school day. It also allows the facilitator an opportunity to discuss and explain the consequences, not only for the pupil involved in constant disruption through talking, but also for the rest of the class including the teacher.

Extension Work

You may want to look at specific listening skills:

- Eye contact.
- Body posture.
- Not interrupting.
- Interested facial expression.
- Acknowledgements, nodding, saying, 'Mmmm,' 'Yes,' and so on.
- Paraphrasing.

There are various models of listening and each contains variations on the above list.

You and a colleague could present a scenario where poor listening skills were being used and use this as a stimulus to generate what good listening skills are.

One- and Two-Way Communications

One-Way

Split the group into pairs and ask them to sit back to back. A is given one of the pictures and B has paper and pencil. A's task is to describe the picture so that B, who cannot see it, can draw it accurately. B cannot ask any questions. When they are finished they can swap roles.

Ask them to compare their pictures and discuss what made communication difficult.

Two-Way

The task is repeated with a new illustration, the only difference is that questions can now be asked. Discuss whether communication was easier.

When the Teacher is Talking

It is usually accepted that when a teacher is talking to the class, pupils need to:

- be quiet

- listen to what the teacher is saying.

This is important because:

- it shows respect to the teacher

- it shows respect to the other pupils

- it gives everyone the chance to hear

- it allows everyone the opportunity to learn.

Basically it allows pupils to hear what is being said and reminds them to pay attention.

Are there times when the teacher is talking that you don't have to listen?

Give examples of when you are supposed to listen:

Give examples of distractions that would prevent you from listening to the teacher:

If the teacher is speaking to the class what should you do?

How does this show respect for the teacher and the other pupils?

The Level of Noise in a Classroom

The noise level in a classroom varies from teacher to teacher and from subject to subject. There are, however, certain situations when teachers want silence and attention from the pupils in the class.

What would it sound like in a classroom if everyone talked at the same time?

Give examples of times at school when you must be completely silent:

Give examples of times at school when you do not have to be completely silent:

What are the signs or clues that you might see or hear from a teacher that would let you know that it is time to keep quiet?

What could or would happen in a classroom if a particular pupil refused to keep quiet?

One-Way Communication

1. Sit back to back with your partner.
2. Don't let your partner see your picture.
3. Describe your picture so your partner can draw it.
4. Do not answer any questions.

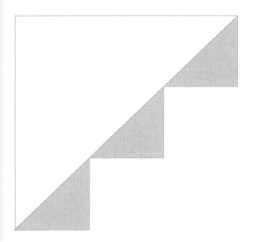

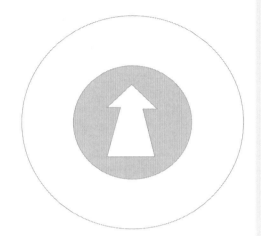

One-Way Communication

1. Sit back to back with your partner.
2. Don't let your partner see your picture.
3. Describe your picture so your partner can draw it.
4. Do not answer any questions.

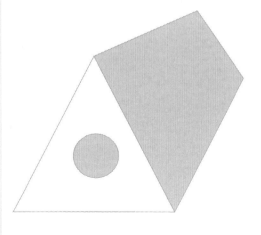

Two-Way Communication

1. Sit back to back with your partner.
2. Don't let your partner see your picture.
3. Describe your picture.
4. You can repeat your instructions.
5. You can answer questions.

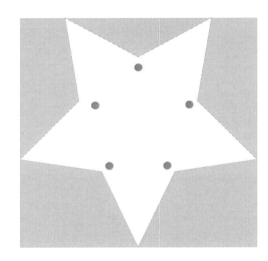

Two-Way Communication

1. Sit back to back with your partner.
2. Don't let your partner see your picture.
3. Describe your picture.
4. You can repeat your instructions.
5. You can answer questions.

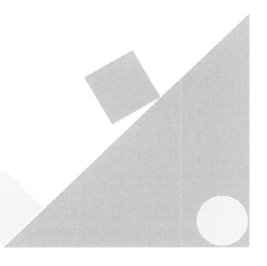

Communication Skills

Activities

Can Talking Cause Trouble?

Talking Can Get Me Into Trouble.

How Do I Get the Teacher's Attention?

A Special Occasion.

Excuses.

Role-Play.

Facilitator Notes

General

It is important to stress to the pupils that communication is a two-way process. There are times during a school day when talking is encouraged but there are also times when talking can be disruptive. Let the pupils work through the examples and lead the discussion during the follow-up.

Can Talking Cause Trouble?

During this activity the pupils are encouraged to consider other pupils. The facilitator should encourage the pupils to look at the timing and appropriateness of talking. Highlight the times and opportunities during the school day when pupils are encouraged to communicate socially.

Talking Can Get Me Into Trouble

During this activity the facilitator asks the pupils to respond to each of the scenarios. During these situations you have information you want to give to someone else but is this the appropriate time? Is it the right time to talk? Is it a time for listening or indeed a time for action? Discuss with the pupils other times when it is inappropriate to talk. Times when talking can be selfish. Times when talking can be a distraction and could lead into a potentially dangerous situation. Emphasise that talking itself is not wrong but when and how you employ it can create a negative time for you.

How Do I Get the Teacher's Attention?

Let the pupils' imagination run riot. Let us look at all the ridiculous and negative ways of getting attention in class. The use of humour by the facilitator in these activities is an important learning strategy. Get the pupils to look at how structured life was in the primary school. In many primary classes it is practice when you have finished your work to line up at the teacher's desk to have your work marked. Everyone knows the system and is happy with it. In post primary it is possible to have different strategies employed by not only each subject department but in fact by each teacher. This can cause confusion for pupils and lead to disruptive situations.

Many of the ideas I obtained from pupils were taken back to teachers and incorporated into whole-school policy.

A Special Occasion

During the next activity it is important that the facilitator directs the discussion. The facilitator explains that the pupil has been invited to an expensive and very popular restaurant. The pupil is asked to fill in the activity page 'A Special Occasion Part 1'.

When the pupils have filled in the response sheet the facilitator leads the discussion on why these conditions apply at the restaurant, how your behaviour affects others and gives the pupils a copy of 'A Special Occasion Part 2'.

After the discussion on the restaurant the pupils are given the activity page on the school situation, 'A Special Occasion Part 3'. The pupils are allowed time to silently read this activity page and are then asked to compare the school responses with the restaurant responses.

Pupils very quickly become aware that school rules of behaviour and what happens outside school in the community are very similar. The facilitator emphasises that learning in school prepares pupils for life after school and that learning is life long.

Excuses

During this activity you are showing that communication must be honest. Using the activity page Excuses, let the pupils tell you about their most outrageous excuses. These situations can be very humorous, strengthen the bond of trust between the facilitator and the pupil, while showing that dishonesty can have a detrimental effect on long-term communication.

Role-Plays

Role-Play 1

The first role-play is between staff. Central to this is the problem of disruption caused by a person wanting immediate answers and attention and not considering the needs of others or indeed that others do have needs. Timing is of the utmost importance. Therefore, prior to starting, the pupils must be on task, on either project work or silent reading. It is important that a teacher is helping a pupil who is experiencing difficulty with the work. The member of staff involved in the disruption must be persistent, must leave the room several times and keep returning with the same interruption. It is important that this is rehearsed beforehand in order for it to appear genuine. When the role-play has finished the facilitator should discuss with the pupils what happened and look at why people in that situation became annoyed. This discussion can then lead into the problems and difficulties caused by persistent pupil disruption in class.

Role-Play 2

This role-play gives pupils an insight into how their disruptive behaviour in class has an effect on other pupils, teachers, and parents. The role-play should last for no more than ten minutes and should be chaired by the facilitator. Before the start of the role-play the facilitator should explain the roles of the characters involved and allow the pupils a few minutes to study and understand their character. When the time is up the facilitator should lead a group discussion using the questions on the observation sheet provided. The observation sheet can be given to the 'audience' so they can focus on the specific points, making notes if relevant.

Can Talking Cause Trouble?

Why do you think that there is a rule about no talking in class?

Why might it bother or annoy other people in the classroom if you were talking?

Would it annoy you if other pupils kept talking when you wanted to hear what the teacher was saying?

During the school day, when can you talk to your friends? List as many examples as you can.

Talking Can Get Me Into Trouble

Look at the following situations. Are these good times to talk to your friends? Think about the possible consequences.

1. You have just sat down for the first period on Monday morning and you start to tell your friend about the exciting time you had at the weekend.
Consequences:

2. You are in P.E. and the teacher is explaining the rules of volleyball to the class. You already know about volleyball so you decide to talk to the pupils beside you about the European Football Match that was on TV last night.
Consequences:

3. The fire bell rings. As you are lining up to leave the room you describe to your friend about the time you visited the Fire Station and had a ride on the Fire Engine.
Consequences:

Talking Can Get Me Into Trouble
(Continued)

4. During the science lesson the teacher is demonstrating a potentially dangerous experiment. You remember that you hadn't told your friend what time you were going to meet outside the youth club that evening, so you tell him.
Consequences:

5. You worked hard during this subject and as a reward the teacher lets you work at the back of the room on a special project. You have a great idea for a poster and discuss it with the pupils beside you.
Consequences:

6. The mathematics teacher is calling out the answers to your homework. Since you have a lot of answers wrong you ask the pupil beside you to explain how to do the questions.
Consequences:

How Do I Get the Teacher"s Attention?

List what you could do that would get you noticed in class. Remember that both positive and negative behaviours will get you attention.

On your list indicate 'trouble for you' and 'good for you'.

Trouble for Me	Good for Me

Can we have an agreed way of getting the teacher's attention?

What are the advantages of having an agreed way of getting the teacher's attention in class?

Does it really matter what the agreed way is?

A Special Occasion, Part 1

The Restaurant

Your favourite aunt and uncle have invited you to a very posh hotel restaurant for a meal to celebrate your birthday.

The table is booked for 7.30pm and the booking had to be made four weeks ago due to the popular demand for this restaurant.

Make comments on each of the following:

Menu

Arriving later than the time you had booked for.

How you would dress for the occasion.

Use of bad or vulgar language at your table.

Very loud talking or shouting at your table.

Not using proper table manners.

A Special Occasion, Part 2

The Restaurant

Situation	Consequences
Arrive at 8.00-8.30	You have lost your table. (Punishment.)
Arrive wearing jeans, tee shirt or trainers	You are not allowed in. (Punishment.)
Cursing/swearing/name-calling.	You will be thrown out. (Punishment.)
Shouting, making a lot of noise, disturbing the peace of others.	Warning – if you continues disturbing the peace of others you will be thrown out. (Punishment.)
Not using proper table manners.	Embarrassment, ridicule (Need for future learning of social skills.)

A Special Occasion, Part 3

School

Is the restaurant similar to school?

Situation	Consequences
Arrive at 9.30-10.00.	You will be placed on detention. (Punishment.)
Arrive without school uniform.	You will be sent home. (Punishment.)
Cursing/swearing/name-calling.	You will be put on detention/sent home/suspended/expelled. (Punishment.)
Shouting, making a lot of noise, disturbing the peace of others.	Warning and if you continue to disturb others you will be put on detention/sent home/suspended/expelled. (Punishment.)
Learning situations (classes).	If you do not make the effort you will not get examinations, gain points and you will have limited choices later on in life.

Excuses

As teachers we often hear excuses for homework not being done, for being late, for not wearing school uniform, for incidents happening in the classroom and so on. Often teachers don't know the entire circumstances surrounding the particular problem but they usually know the pupil.

Examples

I've done my homework but:
- the dog ate it
- someone broke into our house and stole it
- it's like the X-Files – it just disappeared.

I don't have my uniform because:
- my brother/sister wore it to work
- the cat ate it
- it got dirty playing after school so I have to wear my tracksuit instead.

Consider

If someone gives you excuses all the time what would you think about that person?

What are some of the worst excuses that you have heard?

Who is responsible for your uniform?

Who is responsible for your homework?

If you are not careful and lose things, whose responsibility is it?

Role-Play 1

Situation

Teacher 1 is working with an individual pupil.
During the conversation between the teacher and the pupil another member of staff (Teacher 2) approaches and states, 'I want you to look at this.'

The situation that develops shows Teacher 2 persistently interrupting Teacher 1 until Teacher 1 finally tells Teacher 2 that what he wants done is not of immediate importance and could in fact wait until later. A time when both teachers could give the matter their undivided attention.

Notes for Participants

Come together to discuss whether the interruption was necessary. Look at similar situations in the classroom and the concept of self-centredness – our problems are greater than everyone else's and we must get immediate attention.

Role-Play 2: Pupil

Situation

A pupil has been suspended for consistently being disruptive in class. The problem of the pupil's disruptive behaviour has been referred to the form teacher and then the year head. When eventually the pupil was referred to the head teacher, the pupil was given a formal suspension lasting five days.

Before the pupil returns to school the pupil, the parent and the year head meet in order to discuss the pupil's future behaviour.

Pupil

You are in your third year at school and have been having problems in certain classes. You tend to get caught doing 'silly' things in class while other pupils, equally as guilty, tend to get away with it. When chastised by the teacher you get very embarrassed and hide this embarrassment by being aggressive and loud towards the teacher. This type of behaviour has given you a reputation with other pupils and teachers which you now have to respond to.

Role-Play 2: Parent

Situation

A pupil has been suspended for consistently being disruptive in class. The problem of the pupil's disruptive behaviour has been referred to the form teacher and then the year head. When eventually the pupil was referred to the head teacher, the pupil was given a formal suspension lasting five days.

Before the pupil returns to school the pupil, the parent and the year head meet in order to discuss the pupil's future behaviour.

Parent

You want your son to stay at school. You know that he is capable of doing well but because of his present attitude towards school he will not fulfil his full potential. You feel ashamed that your son has acted this way and also feel nervous about the meeting. At home your son is very willing to help and with three younger siblings often takes responsibility for looking after the younger children. You want your son to settle down in school and even though he has promised you in the past that he will settle down, the problems in school seem to be getting worse.

Role-Play 2: Year Head

Situation

A pupil has been suspended for consistently being disruptive in class. The problem of the pupil's disruptive behaviour has been referred to the form teacher and then the year head. When eventually the pupil was referred to the head teacher, the pupil was given a formal suspension lasting five days.

Before the pupil returns to school the pupil, the parent and the year head meet in order to discuss the pupil's future behaviour.

Year Head

This pupil has been referred to you for disruptive behaviour in class. What started as a minor problem has now grown to the point where expulsion from the school may have to be considered. In the past you have talked not only to the pupil but also to the parent. You have tried punishment work and detention. Nothing has worked and you now have several teachers complaining about this pupil's aggressive behaviour and the fact that this pupil is not allowing other pupils to be taught. If it continues, this will affect future grades for other pupils and you have had complaints from several concerned parents.

Role-Play 2: Observation Sheet

Were the issues of the situation discussed in the role-play?

Was enough information exchanged in the role-play?

Did anyone ask for more advice about the situation?

Did they discuss future positive and negative outcomes of the situation?

Was a decision arrived at?

Was the decision difficult to make?

Were there conditions attached to the decision?

Did everyone agree to the decision?

Was there an agreement for future meetings?

Sitting Skills

Activities

Sitting skills.

Movement in the classroom.

Extension work.

Facilitator Notes

Sitting Skills

During this activity the pupils are asked to show how they would sit in various situations. These range from showing that they are interested in what is being said to showing that they are bored and don't want to be involved. Because this is a physical activity the pupils quickly get the meaning of body language. The facilitator should explain how body language can send out the wrong messages. You might be interested in what the teacher is saying and you are paying attention but because you are slouching in your seat your body language is giving the teacher a completely different message.

This is a fun activity and pupils gain a lot of insight from it.

Movement in the Classroom

Pupils are given a copy of the activity page 'Movement in the Classroom' and are given a few minutes to silently look at the examples. The facilitator then instructs the pupils to move in to their group setting for a discussion.

During this activity we are looking at how pupils should move around the room without being a distraction to others. Even though some of the examples may appear to be extreme the pupils will give you other examples even more so. There is a humour in this activity that should not be lost. When pupils laugh at examples of negative behaviours they are starting to learn that some of their own behaviours need to be changed. The grading of the behaviour helps the pupils to understand teachers' responses are differentiated to reflect the severity/level of disruption of the behaviour.

Extension Work

You could discuss how the sitting position affects the brain and is not just boring teachers telling the pupils to sit up straight.

We are bombarded by stimuli and our brains have to make sense of them, some are ignored and others acted upon. We usually only consider the senses of touch, smell, sight, taste and hearing, but we also have a system called the vestibular system and proprioception, which gives us information about our bodies' movement and position in space. The vestibular system maintains the position of the body, particularly the head, in relation to gravity. Proprioceptive receptors let us know about our physical position and give us feedback so we move and keep balance.

The following sitting position helps proprioception and the vestibular system to be balanced and stable, this makes other senses more effective:

- Feet firmly on the floor.
- Back straight.
- Bottom on the rear of the seat of the chair.
- Chair close to the table.
- Hands together on the desk.

So movement, being slumped at the desk, fidgeting, rocking on the chair will reduce attention because the proprioceptive and vestibular systems are bombarding the brain with stimulus about balance and position, so not enough of the brain can concentrate on listening.

Sitting

Ask the pupils to show how they would sit in various situations.

How would you sit in the cinema?

How would you sit in your favourite chair watching TV?

How would you sit if you were tired?

How would you sit if you were bored?

How would you sit to show that you didn't want to listen to someone?

How would you sit to show that you were listening to someone?

How would you sit to show aggression?

How would you sit to show that you were really interested in seeing something?

How do you sit in class?

Discuss body language.

Movement in the Classroom

Pupils need to move around in the classroom.
During a lesson the following pupils have been asked by the teacher to come to the front of the class.
Look at the following situations and decide which pupils are moving properly. Give a score out of 10, with 1 indicating that the pupil is in a lot of trouble and 10 which would be acceptable to all teachers.

Pupil A jumps over the desk.   /10
How do you think the teacher will respond?

....

Pupil B pushes everyone out of the way.   /10
How do you think the teacher will respond?

....

Pupil C makes car noises as he moves around the room.   /10
How do you think the teacher will respond?

....

Pupil D has a chat with everyone he meets.   /10
How do you think the teacher will respond?

....

Pupil E wanders about.   /10
How do you think the teacher will respond?

....

Pupil F moves quietly to the front of the room.   /10
How do you think the teacher will respond?

....

Pupil G kicks every desk on their way.   /10
How do you think the teacher will respond?

....

Pupil H pretends they are an aeroplane and 'zooms' around the room.   /10
How do you think the teacher will respond?

....

Can you give a real example from your experience?

....

Co-Operation

Activities

Sharing.

The Head Teacher.

Happy Times.

Honesty and Respect.

Vandalism.

Friendship: Captain Oates.

Extension Work.

Facilitator Notes

General

When we look at the situations in this session, the important aspect is the development of the concept of respect. Pupils have to be given the opportunity to explore the whole concept and how self-respect, respect for others and property, contributes to gaining respect for themselves.

Sharing

During this activity pupils are seated around a large worktable. Give each pupil one of the Celtic-type pattern which is influenced by the patterns in the Book of Kells and tell them to colour it in without going over the black lines. Each pupil should be given the same six colours. Three of the pencils are taken from each pupil and the remainder are then placed in the middle of the table.

Pupils are asked the question:

'What would you do if you wanted to colour a part of your pattern red and there were no red pencils in the middle?'

The responses are written below with the possible consequences:

- 'I'll take the red one from someone else.' Fighting, therefore classroom disruption. The type of response that got you on to the programme.

- 'I'll wait until someone finishes with the red.' Could be reprimanded by the teacher for not working. Could become bored and start messing about. This strategy could, and more than likely will, lead to problems.

- 'I'll use a different colour.' It is explained that this is the most successful strategy. The teacher at the start did not specify that particular colours must be used. The only stipulation was that colours must be kept within the black lines.

During the colouring in stage the pupils are developing independent silent working skills.

A useful resource for this is The Celtic Colouring Book by Joseph Gervin.

The Head Teacher

In this activity the pupil responds as the head teacher and this allows the facilitator to explore relationships and how these make the pupil feel as a person. Some of the examples will have positive feelings both for the Head teacher and the pupil. Pride in performance, a feeling of achievement, as well as a sharing and recognition of this achievement creates a relationship based on trust. Other examples create aggression and hostility. The facilitator has to help the pupil to explore the contrast in feelings through these examples at the end of which the pupil can decide what type of response and relationship he would prefer to have. It is important during this activity to follow up the examples and guide the pupils to situations where they can see positive benefits for themselves.

Happy Times

Recent past experiences in school, for the majority of pupils on the programme, have been anything but happy. We need to explore the times when these pupils were happy in school and look at the relationships at that time between the pupil and teacher. What was the pupil doing to make these times happy? Again this centres on respect. Self-respect and respect for others. How can we turn the present situation around and look towards a more positive future?

Honesty and Respect

If we allow the pupil to look at situations that are tangible, such as respect for property, we can broaden this into respect for others. It is important that the pupil realises that their negative behaviours in class have an impact on the lives of others.

Vandalism

The examples of vandalism and damage lead us into the area of opportunity lost. By our negative actions we are taking opportunity away from others. Disruption in class means that teaching time has been taken away from pupils who want to learn. The disruptive pupil is taking away other pupils' rights. They are stealing other pupils' opportunities for an education and this can have a long-term effect on future careers. All our actions have an impact, not just on us, but on others in our community.

Friendship

A true friend wants you to do well and will enjoy the praise and glory of your successes. It is important that pupils can discriminate between the values of friendship, peer pressure and selfishness. Captain Oates was thinking of the other members of the group when he made the final sacrifice. He was putting the needs of others before his own. Pupils have to look at the qualities of true friendship and contrast these with the negatives such as selfishness, jealousy, pressure. They have to ask the question, 'Would a true friend want me to be involved in activities that would be negative for me?' It is also important that the facilitator gets the pupil to appraise themselves as a friend to others.

True friends will help you to develop as a person and will celebrate in your successes. These are winning relationships. A losing relationship will not allow you to develop and will involve you in activities that will have a negative effect on you as a person.

Though it is tongue-in-cheek the Carling advertisements showing a group of friends in outer space and an environment like Antarctica might be a useful modern day stimulus to this discussion. They are both on YouTube – search on Carling space advert and Polar Night Out. After reading the story of Captain Oates it might be interesting to discuss if any people would find the Polar Night Out advert in bad taste.

Extension Work

Co-operative group work can be a good vehicle to look at a practical situation rather than a theoretical exercise.

Balloons

Have a group/groups of about five students and give them a task such as create a fantasy creature or a tower or fantastic headwear, and explain that all they will have is 30 balloons, tape and newspaper for their creation. They are to work as a team. Give them five minutes' planning time and then give out the materials and allow 10-15 minutes for the task.

When they have finished, discuss the practicalities. Did they co-operate, what was difficult, what was hard?

Newspaper

A variation is just to give newspaper and tape to create

- a freestanding structure as tall as possible
- a bridge as long as possible that will support the weight of six pencils.

When they have finished, discuss the practicalities. Did they co-operate, what was difficult, what was hard?

Sharing

© Karl Designs

The Head Teacher

You are the head teacher of the school. Consider the following students and decide how you might respond.

Pupil A: My teacher has sent me to you for not doing my homework. I don't intend doing it and I will not do it.
Response:

Pupil B: My form teacher has sent me down to show you my project. I was awarded an A*.
Response:

Pupil C: I was caught fighting on the bus but it's OK because I won.
Response:

Pupil D: The P.E. teacher sent me down to show you the medal I won at the Area Athletics Championships.
Response:

Pupil E: I don't have to do what you want. My dad is a lawyer and we'll sue you.
Response:

Pupil F: You have no right to take my rings. They are my property. If I want to wear them I will and you can't stop me.
Response:

Happy Times

Different things make different people happy. It may be an event we have been looking forward to for a long time. It may be something that happens unexpectedly.

In Ancient China there was a writer who made a list of things that made him feel happy. He called it 'The 33 Happy Moments'.
Two of these were:
1. Opening a window to let a wasp out of the room.
2. Cutting a green watermelon with a sharp knife on a summer's day.

Make a list of the various things in school that have made you happy.

Make a list of the various things in school that would make your teacher happy.

Tell us about any happy moments that you had in school that have stayed in your memory.

Honesty and Respect

We expect others to respect our property and valuables.
We would like to think that other people would leave our valuables alone.
We could trust other people.
Other people would be honest.

Do we set the same standards for ourselves?
Do we respect other people's property?
Do we respect other people's valuables?

Look at the following situations:
1. During P.E. a pupil does not hand the teacher his valuables. After the lesson his
   money, watch and bus ticket are missing.
Comment on the feelings involved:

2. A pupil finds £20 in the school playground and takes it to the head teacher.
Comment on the feelings involved:

3. You have lost an envelope with £15 in it. This money was to pay for a school trip.
   You had the money in your pocket during registration but now during the second
   period, when the teacher is collecting the money, you cannot find the envelope
Comment on the feelings involved:

4. As you are walking down a corridor you see another pupil sneaking around the P.E.
   changing rooms. It looks as if she is stealing from other pupils.
Comment on the feelings involved:

5. What would your feelings be if you found that:
Someone had stolen your pencils?

Someone had cut the straps from your schoolbag?

Your bus pass has gone missing?

Respect

Being disruptive in class is stealing other people's time.
It is stealing other people's opportunity.
It is stealing other people's future.

Vandalism

We all like to work in an area that is clean, bright and comfortable. We expect other people to respect and look after our property. Study the following and give your comments:

1. You sit on a chair and your new trousers are ruined because someone put chewing gum on the seat.
Comment including feelings:

2. You go into a room, which is covered in litter, and the desks have graffiti written on them.
Comment including feelings:

3. An important visitor comes to our school. What would the person think if they saw papers and rubbish lying on the corridors and slogans written on the walls and desks?
Comment including feelings

4. How would you show respect for our school?
Comment:

5. The cost of cleaning and repairing can take away other opportunities that could have been purchased with the money.
Comment:

6. Graffiti and slogans written on walls and desks usually put someone down.
Comment:

7. People who vandalise materials, instruments or other resources are taking away, from others, the opportunity to use these.
Comment:

Friendship: Captain Oates

In 1910 the famous British explorer, Captain Scott, led an expedition which attempted to be the first to reach the South Pole. Unfortunately they suffered many delays on the way and this not only meant that their rival, Roald Amundsen, got to the Pole first but also by the time they did get there the worst of the Antarctic weather was beginning. On the way back Scott's party was dogged by bad weather, they were short of provisions and were making slow progress. One of the party, Captain Oates, was particularly badly affected. Oates' frostbite was so bad that he could scarcely walk and had to slit his sleeping bag almost to the base in order to fit his swollen feet in. He knew that there were not enough provisions for all of them and he also knew that he was slowing up the rest of the expedition. On 17 March 1912, his 32nd birthday, they were all sheltering in their tent from a raging blizzard. Oates knew, and everyone else knew, that nobody could last for long outside in those terrible conditions. He got up from his sleeping bag and said to the others, 'I am going outside and I may be gone some time.' He went outside, disappeared into the blizzard, sacrificing his life for his friends, and was never seen again.

Discuss the real nature of friendship:
- Faithful.
- Reliable.
- Sacrifice.
- Supportive.
- Pride in others' achievements.

Discuss the negative aspects of friendships:
- Glue sniffing.
- Drugs.
- Stealing.
- Joy riding.
- Causing damage.
- Drinking alcohol.

Are the people who want us to engage in these behaviours real friends?

In the negative friendship:
- You are being used.
- They are selfish.
- You are being made a fool of.
- They are jealous of you.
- They put pressure on you.

Winning relationships or losing relationships?

Individual Work Skills

Projects

Advertising Company.

Fantasy Creatures.

Autobiography.

Creepy House.

Facilitator Notes

General

The following projects have been designed in order that pupils can develop a more positive attitude towards their work in school. The main aims of these projects are to build self-esteem, confidence, produce work that can be publicly displayed and to motivate pupils.

There must be strict rules and regulations for these pieces of work:

- The work must be clean and tidy.
- The acceptable standard is set by the teacher.
- The work will only be displayed if it meets the teacher's standard.
- Work will be repeated if it does not reach the required standard.

This will be the first time that some pupils have completed a piece of work. It may be the first time they can be proud of achieving, having been motivated to learn, and may be the first time they have taken work home. It can be a new experience for them to have work displayed in class, being the only time they have succeeded in completing a piece of work, but this achievement can motivate pupils into wanting more success through learning. When pupils are getting their work ready for presentation word processing can enhance the final project. During the project work pupils are developing independent study skills. In several of the projects oral communication skills are high on the priority list of developmental skills.

The following are examples only and other more appropriate projects can be used.

The techniques for presentation of the projects are paper and print. If appropriate, especially for the 'Advertising Company', a PowerPoint presentation would be an alternative technique.

Advertising Company

There are two projects under the heading 'Advertising Company':

1. Glen Castle.
2. Glen Tour Company.

The facilitator should pick whichever one will have most interest for the particular group of pupils. In order to motivate and stimulate the pupils the facilitator should show examples of marketing leaflets and brochures on local places of interest. The pupils are then told that, individually, they are marketing companies trying to win this advertising campaign. Each pupil has to produce a marketing leaflet, booklet, on an A4 page folded in half. To ensure that each booklet is of the highest standard possible all writing should be done on separate pages in order that spelling and grammar corrections can be applied before entry to the finished piece of work. Each pupil should have an individual desk to work at but a communal table should be used for drawing and colouring. During this activity pupils are encouraged to develop individual working habits but also to develop skills that will enable them to work independently at a group table while at the same time moving between individual and group tables without disturbing the work of other pupils.

At the finish of the advertising projects the pupils are required to do a verbal presentation on their proposed marketing package. The presentation is timed for two minutes and is followed by questions, from the facilitator and other adults present, on the presentation. All pupils and staff will then vote on which pupil (company) should get the advertising contract. This should be based on the standard of the brochure produced and the verbal presentation.

Fantasy Creatures

During this activity pupils have to use their imagination. Starting with a drawing of their creature the pupil then builds up a profile of how the creature lives and what it does. The information the pupil has gathered is then used in a story where their fantasy creature is the central figure. Finally the drawing, the background information and the story are arranged to make a poster.

This project helps the pupils to develop individual work skills, work with others in a shared area, learn how to move around the room without disturbing others and produce a piece of work they can be proud of. When the pupils are writing they should be seated at an individual desk but for drawing and colouring they should be at a shared table with shared resources.

My Autobiography

The facilitator starts this project showing copies of autobiographies by sports people, pop stars and celebrities, and emphasises that an autobiography is the life story of the author. It is important that the facilitator stresses the point that each individual pupil is as important a person as the people in these selected autobiographies. We all have talents and abilities and it is important that we recognise these, develop them, and use our abilities to their maximum. We all have our own story to tell and our autobiography to write.

Creepy House

At the start of this session the facilitator gives each pupil a drawing of a house and a list of questions. The pupils are told that there are no right or wrong answers to these questions and that they have to use their imagination in order to find answers. During this project pupils will be working on independent silent working skills. When pupils are doing written work this is done at their own desks, while drawings and colouring in are done at a group area where they have to share pencils and colouring pens. When pupils have finished their story the facilitator can help them correct spelling and grammar before the pupil spends some time on the final presentation for display.

Advertising Company – Glen Castle

Brief

To design a brochure that would encourage people to visit Glen Castle.

Background

The owner of the castle wants to turn it into a tourist attraction.

Special Interests

A haunted bedroom.
Knights and armour.
Underground secret passages
Moat House Café.

Additional Information

Prices:
Child under 15yrs £2.50
Adult £4.00
Family Ticket (2A+2C) £10.00.

Opening Hours:

Monday-Friday 11.00am-5.00pm.
Saturday-Sunday 9.00am-8.00pm.

Hints:

Do all work in rough.
Think of the layout design.
Final brochure is all about presentation.

When the booklet is finished each company will do a verbal presentation followed by interview questions, from adults, on their presentation.

Glen Castle

The following layout might be helpful but don't let this restrict your creative talents!

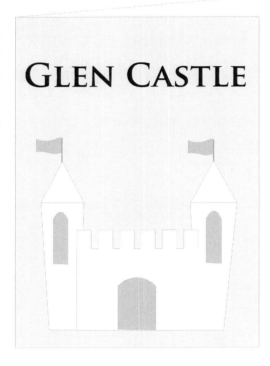

GLEN CASTLE

INFORMATION

PRICES

MENU

ADMISSIONS

OPENING TIMES
WEB ADDRESS
EMAIL ADDRESS

LIST OF
ATTRACTIONS

INFORMATION

STORY OF
HAUNTED
BEDROOM

KNIGHTS AND
ARMOUR

BATTLES

SECRET PASSAGES

Advertising Company – Glen Tour Company

Brief

To design a brochure that would encourage people to use the Glen Tour Company.

Background

The owner wants to highlight his business as a luxury tour company.

Special Interests

Luxury coaches.
TV.
Video.
Air Conditioning.
Roomy.
Expert Couriers.
Toilets.

Additional Information

National and European destinations.
Low prices.
Luxury hotels.

Hints

Do all work in rough.
Think of the layout design.
Final brochure is all about presentation.

When the booklet is finished each company will do a verbal presentation followed by interview questions, from adults, on their presentation.

Glen Tour Company

The following layout might be helpful but don't let this restrict your creative talents!

GLEN TOUR COMPANY

INFORMATION

PRICES

WHO CAN BE CONTACTED

LOCATION

WEB ADDRESS

EMAIL ADDRESS

LIST OF SPECIAL FEATURES

INFORMATION

DESCRIPTION OF LUXURY COACHES

WHERE YOU CAN GO - NATIONAL AND EUROPEAN

Fantasy Creatures

For thousands of years people have used their imaginations to invent new creatures. Not content with the wide variety of animals in nature people have told stories of fantastic creatures that at times have magical or mystical powers.

One of these creatures was the phoenix. This huge, brightly coloured bird was supposed to spend its life flying around the sun and to live for 500 years. At any one time there was only one phoenix in existence and it was a male bird.
When its 500-year life was at an end the phoenix made a nest of fragrant spices and twigs which was set on fire by the sun's rays. The phoenix sat on the nest and fanned the fire with its large wings until the flames burnt it.
The following day a new young and beautiful phoenix arose out of the ashes of the dead fire.

Other fantasy creatures were the basilisk, the griffin, the sphinx, the dragon, the unicorn, the centaur and the mermaid.

These fantasy creatures were not just in past times. In our own time we have fantasy creatures such as the Loch Ness Monster and the Abominable Snowman.

Invent your own fantasy creature. Give it a name. Make a coloured drawing of it. Describe how and where it lives. Describe what it eats and drinks. Describe any unusual habits that it has. Write a story in which your fantasy creature is the central figure.

Using all of this information, make an educational poster on your creature.

My Autobiography

An autobiography is the story of a person's life.

Thousands of people, not only the famous, have written their autobiographies. There are recent examples of sports people, pop stars and politicians.

Let us look at how we would write your autobiography.

The following is a writing frame or plan for you to follow. It will help you to organise your life story.

Chapter 1 The Background.

Describe your family, what your parents/carers are like, their appearance and their personalities. What about grandparents, brothers or sisters? Write about where you were born and where you live. You could write a paragraph on each of the following: your room, your house, your area, your country.

Chapter 2 The Beginnings

What are your earliest memories?
What were you like as a baby or small child?
Have you any stories to tell?

Chapter 3 Education

Describe your time at primary school.
If you remember you could write about your first day.
Describe your successes and disappointments.
Describe the friends you made and your teachers.
Have you any interesting stories to tell?

Describe your time at secondary school.
If you remember you could write about your first day.
Describe your successes and disappointments.
Describe the friends you made and your teachers.
Have you any interesting stories to tell?

Chapter 4 A Special Event.

It could be a family or school day out, a family holiday, wedding, first communion, confirmation.
Try to explain how you felt at the time.
What was the atmosphere of the occasion?
Why does this event stand out as special in your memory?

Chapter 5 Important People

Choose two or three of the most important and influential people in your life.
Describe them.
Write about why they were so important.

Chapter 6 Character

What do you look like?
What are your good points and bad points?
What are your strengths and weaknesses?
Describe your appearance and personality.

Chapter 7 The Future

What about your future?
What are your hopes and ambitions?
What about your next few years in secondary school?

Creepy House

Study the picture of the house, then write the answers to these questions:

- What do you think the house is called?
- Who do you think lives in the house?
- Why do you think the downstairs window is broken?
- Who might go to the house during the day?
- Why do you think there is a hole in the roof?
- Who might visit the house at night?
- Can you see something in the window above the door? Who or what might it be?
- Do you think there are any animals in the house?
- Why is the garden overgrown?
- Is that a light in the upstairs room?
- Who or what might be there?
- What are they doing?
- Why is there a cross in the front garden?

- What do you think happened?
- What is at the front door?
- If you rang the bell who would answer?
- When the full moon is shining what do you think happens in the house?

Use the above questions and your answers to help you write a story about the house. Using your imagination and visuals might be a useful technique to create the story.

The Final Session

Activities

Evaluation.

Celebration and Graduation.

Programme Review Meeting.

Facilitator Notes

Evaluation

The final session of the programme should be a time for group evaluation. Teachers and pupils should discuss in an informal setting what has been gained from completing the programme. I have found that more is achieved if this meeting is conducted sitting in easy chairs and accompanied by tea and biscuits than having a formal meeting where the teacher and pupil are separated by a desk.

What new skills have been learned and what choices have been decided upon? Individual pupils should look at what difficulties will be involved in returning to the mainstream class and how they can be supported in overcoming these difficulties. On the sheet 'Future Behavioural Objectives' the pupil evaluates progress made during the programme and suggests targets that are hoped to be achieved in the near future. With the help and encouragement of the facilitator these behavioural targets must be realistic, specific to the pupils needs, attainable by the pupil and have time restraints. 'During the first week back in class I will get to class on time, I will not leave my seat without permission and I will not shout out in class.' Because these targets have been developed by the pupil, with guidance from the facilitator, the pupil has ownership of the targets and is therefore empowered to show improvement.

Celebration and Graduation

The final session should also be a time for celebration. I always finished the programme with a feel-good graduation. It is important that the head teacher, assistant head teacher or a member of the Board of Governors attends this graduation and emphasises to the pupils what they have achieved and stress the faith we have for their future achievements. A certificate could be presented to the pupil. It is amazing what a small amount of praise, a slice of celebration cake, a soft drink and an informal positive meeting with authority figures can do for these pupils self-esteem and hope for the future.

Programme Review Meeting

At the end of the programme, before returning to class, the teacher, the carer, and the pupil meet in order to evaluate the progress made by the pupil and agree on a way forward. It is important that positive advances made by the pupil during the programme are highlighted and realistic expectations for the future are discussed. The sheet 'Choice Programme Review' is designed for the carer, the school and the pupil to make comments on aspects of the pupil's improvement during the programme. It must be stressed that completion of the programme does not mean that every pupil will suddenly return to mainstream class and become a model pupil. During the programme an opportunity has developed that allows the school, the carer and the pupil to work in closer partnership, and this must be further developed if meaningful future progress is to be made by the pupil and for the pupil.

Future Behavioural Objectives

1. ....

   ....

   ....

2. ....

   ....

   ....

3. ....

   ....

   ....

Pupil's signature: ....

Teacher's signature: ....

Review date: ....

Pupil Evaluation

Choice Programme Review

Pupil: ....

Date: ....

Present: ....

Progress on the Programme: ....

Targets for the immediate future:

1. ....

   ....

2. ....

   ....

3. ....

   ....

Parent/Carer Comments: ....

....

Pupil Comments: ....

....

Staff Comment: ....

....

Certificate of Merit

....

has successfully completed the

Choice Programme.

Areas of study included:

Concentration skills.

Communication skills.

Listening skills.

Co-operative skills.

Individual project work.

Signed ....

Date ....

Chapter 6

After the Programme

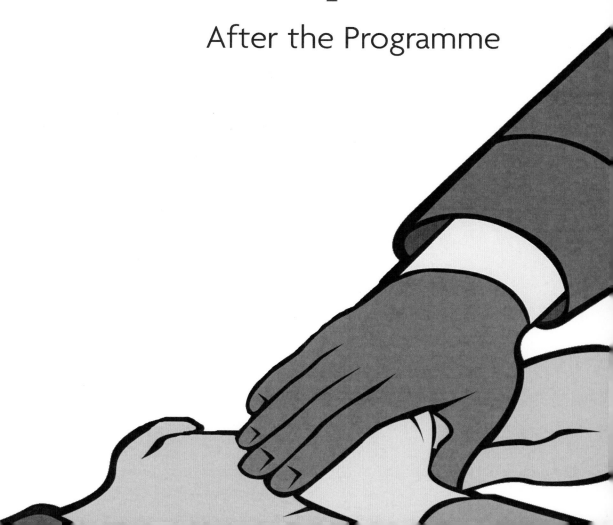

Chapter 6 After the Programme

The programme has given the pupil the opportunity to look at their personal situation within the school environment and to make positive choices about their future. In order to help the pupil develop within the school environment support strategies must be put into place by the programme staff. These strategies could include:

- the use of support staff
- merit awards
- time outs
- behaviour support periods
- target diaries.

The Use of Support Staff

Well-trained, motivated and conscientious support staff are a positive asset to any school. These staff can form more informal relations with pupils that can be beneficial to pupils on the Choice Programme. Before a pupil enters the programme support staff can provide invaluable information by observing the pupil during those classes that are causing most concern. During the programme they can form an informal positive relationship with a pupil that is often not possible for teachers to achieve. Due to this, support staff are often excellent mentors both during and after the programme.

Merit Awards

Two types of merit award schemes are commonly used in schools. Some schools use a system whereby each pupil starts with maximum points and can lose points during the course of a school day. This is a very negative approach where pupils are not motivated to do well since the system is designed to penalise or take away points. If you start with maximum points you cannot improve, you can only go down, you can only lose. The system whereby each pupil starts from a zero base and gains points is more positive and motivational for pupils. When pupils have returned to class, after the programme, and with the aid of a target diary, their targets can be incorporated into the scheme and therefore become motivational by gaining points for the pupil. In order for this to happen staff must embrace a whole-school positive behaviour strategy that is consistent across all aspects of school life.

For the majority of pupils the programme and the relevant support strategies will be enough to guarantee that the pupil remains within the mainstream class and will achieve positive results from a post primary education. For a minority of pupils the programme will have to be revisited. Aspects of the programme relevant to the pupil will have to be further developed. This should not be seen as a failure of the programme but that a long journey consists of a lot of small steps and we must always remind ourselves and our staff that the pupil has not changed overnight into a perfect pupil.

Time Outs

After a pupil has completed the programme and returned to class, it must be remembered that he has not been transformed into a perfect pupil. He has decided to make positive choices but there can be times when he slips back into his previous behaviours. He might feel frustrated and angry, someone might be winding him up or there might be pressures from outside school, and it is during such times that he needs a time out. In basketball terms a time out is usually taken when the game is not going the way of the team. The time out allows the coach and the players an opportunity to reappraise the situation and introduce tactics to turn the game in their favour. This is also true for the pupil. A time out, whether it is for one period or one day, allows the pupil and the facilitator time to look at what has been achieved in order to reappraise the current situation and plan for changes that will be more positive for the future.

Behaviour Support Periods

When a pupil has completed the programme and returned to class the hard work is only starting for that pupil. There will be times when she does not live up to her own expectations and when she feels the effort she is making is not being recognised by teachers. It is vital that during the initial weeks back in class the pupil is supported by programme staff. During this period the group of pupils who completed the course together should meet on a weekly basis, with their mentor, to discuss how their lives are progressing in school. This forms a self-help group where pupils can share experiences and offer advice to each other with the guidance of a mentor. The group becomes motivational for the individual pupil.

The individual pupil, on a weekly basis, should meet with their programme mentor and talk through how the week has worked out.

For most pupils the behaviour support periods usually last for a period of one month after completion of the programme, but for some pupils, this can last longer. If a pupil needs the support in order to remain in class then the support should be given.

Target Diary

The target diary is a contract or agreement between the school, the home and the pupil. The school agrees to:

- help the pupil settle in a mainstream class
- provide support and advice
- encourage and motivate and offer time out when difficult situations might arise
- establish with the support of the carer and the pupil a personal education plan that will establish a way forward.

Finally to monitor and report the pupil's progress, by means of the target diary, to the carer.

The carer agrees to:

- monitor the diary daily
- discuss with the pupil how they are coping in school

- encourage and praise the pupil on progress made

- contact the school immediately should any difficulties arise.

The pupil agrees to keep the targets stated in the diary. The pupil also agrees to meet with a member of staff at the end of each school day to discuss remarks made in the diary. If any difficulties should arise the pupil agrees to immediately report to a designated teacher before a major incident develops.

The three targets agreed must be graded in terms of difficulty to obtain. The first target should be relatively easy to manage, for example:

- Arrive at school on time.

- Wear a school uniform.

- Attend all classes.

- Sit at the front of the room.

The other two targets should be curricular and behavioural.

- Raise my hand if I have a point to make.

- Complete the task set by the teacher.

After each week's completion of the target diary the programme teacher and the pupil decide on whether the pupil should go off the diary or continue for another week. New targets can be set for each new week.

It should be noted that for some pupils the target diary becomes an essential part of their school life. It becomes their excuse, their prop, for future behaviour in school. I have experienced pupils who have by their own choice stayed on a target diary weeks, even months, after the school recommended they could do without it. It gave the pupil an excuse, a get out clause and saved them face with their peers when they wouldn't get involved in any disruption. These pupils have made positive choices and the target diary gives them a legitimate excuse in front of their mates.

Finally

The Choice Programme, developing a whole-school ethos of positive behaviour, creating strong partnerships with families, and open communication with and between external agencies, gives us greater choices in helping each individual child overcome difficulties and make the maximum use of their time at school. That is the learning environment that I as a teacher want to teach in. That is why I chose teaching as a profession, I wanted to work with and help young people to achieve their potential.

Target Diary

Name: ....

Class: ....

Year Head: ....

Week Beginning: ....

Pupil

In order to help me stay in a mainstream class I agree to work towards the targets that are set for my behaviour.
Pupil signature:
Date:

Parent

In order to help my son/daughter make the most of his/her educational opportunities at school and keep him/her in a mainstream class I agree to check the targets on a daily basis.

Parent signature:
Date:

School

In order to help stay in a mainstream class we will monitor his/her behaviour by use of the target diary, on a daily basis, and keep in contact with the pupil and the parent.
Teacher signature:
Date:

Subject Teacher

The pupil will give you the target diary at the start of each period. At the end of each period tick each target met. There is a space for positive comments.

This week's targets are:

1 ....

....

2 ....

....

3 ....

....

I will try my best to meet these targets.

Signed: ....

Date ....

Remember: This diary is your responsibility.

Target Diary

Day:

Target 1

Target 2

Target 3

Comments

Teacher	Target 1	Target 2	Target 3	Comments

Year Head:

Pupil:

Pupil Signature:

Parent Signature:

Bibliography

Bell, D. (2005) *Annual Report of Her Majesty's Chief Inspector of Schools*. Ofsted.

Charlton, T. & David, K. (1993) *Managing Misbehaviour in Schools* (2nd ed.). London: Routledge.

Cheminias, R. (2006) *Every Child Matters: A Practical Guide for Teachers*. London: David Fulton Publishers Limited.

Department of Education, Northern Ireland. (DE) (1997/1998) *Education and Training Inspection* Report. Bangor, N.I.: Department of Education.

DfEE (1997) *Excellence for All Children: Meeting Special Educational Needs*. DfEE Publications. London: The Stationery Office.

DfEE (1999) *Disadvantaged Youth: A Critical Review of the Literature on Scope, Strategies and Solutions*. Research paper 169. London: The Stationery Office.

Epstein, J. (2001) *Schools, Family and Community Partnerships*. Boulder, CO: Westview Press.

Epstein, J. & Salinas, K. (2004) *Partnering with Families and Communities*. Education Leadership. Vol 61, No 8.

Gervin, J. (1995) *The Celtic Colouring Book*. Cork, Ireland: Ossian Publications Ltd.

Goleman, D. (1995) *Emotional Intelligence*. New York: Bantam Books.

Greenham, G. (1989) *The Book of Kells Colouring Book*. Cork, Ireland: Ossian Publications Ltd.

Hutchings, J. & Bywater, T. (2007) *Parenting intervention in Sure Start Services for children at risk of developing Conduct Disorder: pragmatic randomised controlled trial*. BMJ, 334:678.

Morris, R., Reid, E. & Fowler, J. (1993) *Education Act 1993: A Critical Guide*. Association of Metropolitan Authorities.

National Strategy (2005) *Behaviour and Attendance Toolkits*, Key Stage 3. London: DfES.

National Strategy (2005) *Social and Emotional Aspects of Learning: Improving Behaviour, Improving Learning*. London: DCSF ref: 0110-2005.

National Strategy (2009) *Promoting and Supporting Positive Behaviour in Primary Schools: Developing Social and Emotional Aspects of Learning (SEAL)*. London: DCSF ref: 00153 – 2009 FLY-EN.

Ofsted (2005) *Managing Challenging Behaviour*. London: HMI 2363.

Primary National Strategy (2004) *Promoting Social, Emotional and Behaviour Skills in Primary Schools*. London: DfES.

Salovey, P. & Mayer, J. D. (1990) *Emotional Intelligence. Imagination, Cognition, and Personality*. New York: Harper.

Secondary Strategy (2005) *Social and Emotional Behaviour Skills*. London: DfES.

Slee, R. (1995) *Changing Theories and Practices of Discipline*. London: Falmer Press.

Steer, Sir Alan (2005) *Report of the Practitioners' Group on School Behaviour and Discipline*. London: DCSF ref: 1950 – 2005DOC-EN.

Visser, J. (2003) *A Study of Children and Young People who Present Challenging Behaviour*. University of Birmingham. Ofsted.

Watkins, C. (2000) *Managing Classroom Behaviour: from Research to Diagnosis*. London: Institute of Education, University of London.